Sagacity

1/10

Robin –

Thanks for allowing the seniors
to share their wisdom
with you !!

Max Fuentes Fuhrmann
PhD

Sagacity

◆

What I Learned From My Elderly Psychotherapy Clients

By Max E. Fuhrmann, Ph.D.,
Clinical Psychologist,
as told to Jeff Shevlowitz

iUniverse, Inc.
New York Lincoln Shanghai

Sagacity
What I Learned From My Elderly Psychotherapy Clients

iUniverse books may be ordered through booksellers or by contacting:

iUniverse
2021 Pine Lake Road, Suite 100
Lincoln, NE 68512
www.iuniverse.com
1-800-Authors (1-800-288-4677)

ISBN-13: 978-0-595-40597-8 (pbk)
ISBN-13: 978-0-595-84963-5 (ebk)
ISBN-10: 0-595-40597-5 (pbk)
ISBN-10: 0-595-84963-6 (ebk)

Printed in the United States of America

Contents

Acknowledgments

I wish to acknowledge the constructive and helpful comments of Patrick Barker, Ph.D., Patricia Clute, R.N., Dolores Gallagher, Ph.D., Margaret Gatz, Ph.D., Claudine Griggs, M.A., Steven G. Holston, Ph.D., Scott R. Jones, M.S.W., M.S.G., M.B.A., L.C.S.W., Bob Knight, Ph.D., Patric Magee, B.A., Nan Renaud, B.A., Debra Sheets, R.N., Ph.D. and Larry Thompson, Ph.D. Each took time out of their busy careers and lives to read chapters.

I also want to pay homage to my many senior clients, without whose stories, I would have never felt inspired to write this book. My current clients continued to prod me with questions about this book's release, indicating a great deal of interest in reading it, which kept me going through bouts of stagnation.

Additionally, I want to thank my partner and spouse of almost twenty years, Bette Fuhrmann, R.N., Ph.D., without whom, I would not have had the courage to take time out of my career to write it. She has been a cheerleader and wise sage who has never wavered in her support of me.

Lastly, I want to acknowledge my "co-author" and friend, Jeff Shevlowitz. Mr. Shevlowitz is also the author of Abiding Hope: Bearing Witness to the Holocaust. I was so moved by this book about a holocaust survivor and by other plays he has written that I feel honored that he took the time to grace my stories with his heartfelt writing ability.

Foreword

Will Rogers once said, "Good judgment comes from experience and a lot of that comes from bad judgment."

Can you imagine the number of stories Will Rogers had to tell, the number of experiences he had to have, before he found the wisdom of those words? Good judgment is a life's work, and is based upon a life's worth of experiences. When a person lives a long life they become a storyteller looking for the right audience. Often the right audience takes time to find. But when an aged storyteller and the right audience find each other they create a whole new story to tell. This is the story of <u>Sagacity: What I Learned From My Elderly Psychotherapy Clients</u>.

At one time in history elder storytellers were considered the wise people of the community. Today we live in an age of experts and the wisdom an older individual has gained over a lifetime of experience is easily dismissed as unimportant. Wisdom does not compete well against scientifically based knowledge and expertise. Time becomes merely one more commodity in modern life. It is not accepted as appropriate to waste that valuable commodity listening to the elderly. Wisdom conveyed by story telling appears to be inefficient. Scientific experts are more practical, direct, and to the point. Storytellers tease their audience into uncertainty over meaning and offer no clear answers. Scientific experts provide their audience with advice for immediate use. Their advice can direct behavior. Storytelling suggests feelings and ideas but the lessons learned from a story can take time. For example, how old where you when you finally understood the lessons taught by your parents when they told you their stories of their childhood? Are you like me, still wondering about the meaning of a particular story? Or, did we find their stories to be a waste of our time?

Our media based culture permits us to reduce the status of storytelling to a form of entertainment and fantasy. It is assumed that stories are not told to share information. Storytelling is a method of information exchange that is too uncertain, while the ambiguity of metaphor and allegory cause confusion. We prefer useful information from informed people, presented to us emphatically and quickly. After all, experts use fact-based data from empirical research to inform and guide our future decision-making. A storyteller takes us back in time and to other places, sometimes revealing a secret. But is the knowledge gained from storytelling reliable? Valued expert advice is based on knowledge. Yet knowledge alone fails to improve our judgment. Stories can create an internal foundation upon which we find the strength to alter our judgment.

The ingredients of a life-changing story are easily collected in a brief moment in time. Yet some people's stories can take a lifetime to be told. Sometimes, when stories are told the meaning can be hidden from the audience and sometimes the meaning of a story is even concealed from the storyteller. This is the subtext of any given story. This is where wisdom, and frustrating ambiguity are found. On occasion when the story has taken a lifetime to be revealed and finally spoken it is because it may have taken a lifetime for the storyteller to find the right audience to hear the tale.

In each chapter of <u>Sagacity</u> we find a psychotherapist providing his usual and customary expertise and therapeutic services for an older adult client. Each client has an intriguing story to tell. As an expert in the field, the clinical psychologist-gerontologist has extensive academic education and training for this work. As each story unfolds he discovers there are unexpected outcomes that take him beyond his academic and clinical expertise. While the storyteller always takes center stage in each chapter the focus of the story will change. As each older adult tells their story we find that the authors have a story to tell as well. By listening to their stories, the therapist becomes a part of the story. He finds wisdom beyond mere expertise. More importantly, he allows himself to alter his preconceptions and become the student as much as the teacher.

Scott R. Jones, M.S.W, M.S.G., M.B.A., L.C.S.W.
Director of Family Court Services
Ventura, California 2006

Preface

Very early in my career as a clinical psychologist working with the elderly, I realized that I was learning a great deal about life, relationships, loss and acceptance from my clients. Sometimes, I feared that I was learning more from the clients than they were from me. This was not something that I had anticipated, nor had any instructor during my years in school mentioned it. These individuals, in dealing with illness, crisis, death, and isolation, exhibited coping mechanisms that can only be considered to be astonishing in their depth and complexity.

I began my career with the expectation that I would be able to impact the quality of life for my clients. I like to feel that I have accomplished that goal, to a greater or lesser extent. What I did not expect was the impact that my clients would have on the quality of *my* life.

Dealing with my clients over the years, I have learned lessons that have severed me well in every facet of my life. In the following stories, I hope that you, too, will be able to appreciate what can be learned from sharing life experiences with those who have successfully dealt with the best, and worst, that life has to offer.

When asked to provide written permission to use their stories, some clients were shocked that their stories would be of any value to others. Sadly, this supports the idea that the old of today do not believe that they have any wisdom to offer to the young or to each other.

Despite having permission, I still wanted to ensure the privacy of my clients. I have synthesized the most important aspects of several cases. I have used fictitious names and places, as well as changing most of the specifics. I have also combined characteristics of several cases into one narrative. What has not been altered in any way is the basic decency and humanity of my clients as well as the lessons I was fortunate enough to be able to learn from them.

In reading the following chapters, I can only hope that you may be able to come to appreciate my elderly clients as I have learned to do. I hope that the value of the wisdom they have gained over their years will not be lost. They shared it with me, and I, in turn, am sharing with you, for I have also learned from them that wisdom is more valuable when shared.

Indomitable

I glanced at the clock in my new office. My first appointment of the day, Natalie, was due in less than fifteen minutes. One thing I had learned while working with seniors during my internship was that they were seldom late. When they were late, the first thing they did was to apologize for being late.

I was determined that I would be able to project the air of confidence, and competence, that I had observed worked best with clients, and the seniors in particular. To prepare, I reread what little I knew of Natalie from our brief conversation when she set the appointment earlier in the week.

Natalie was depressed. "Anguish" was the actual word she had used. She was in her late 80's, still healthy and self-sufficient. She had mentioned the death of her son, her only child. Her voice had been clear and direct, with no evidence of the hesitation or slight shaking many people expect from those in advanced age.

The information in my notes wasn't extensive, but it left me with a sense that Natalie would be little different from the majority of seniors I had dealt with on my way becoming licensed as a clinical psychologist. Another glance at the clock and, as if on cue, the small light on the wall flashed, indicating the arrival of the client in the waiting room.

Opening the door, I welcomed Natalie into the office. She was not what I expected. Of medium height, she was dressed in a conservative pantsuit with a flower-patterned blouse. At close to 90 years old, she had driven herself to the office for our appointment and projected an air of assurance and self-reliance. Yet, as I held out my hand to welcome her, I couldn't help but notice that her eyes appeared devoid of emotion.

She shook my hand, studying me more keenly than I was evaluating her. "You look a lot younger than I imagined from your voice. How long have you been in practice?"

"Several years," I hedged. While, to be honest, I had been licensed for less than a year, in order to get to that point I had indeed spent several years in study and internship.

"I think I have socks older than you," she commented as she sat in the chair I offered to her. "How old *are* you?"

1

I could feel my back stiffen slightly as I became defensive, but before I said anything, I saw a sparkle in her eyes and an upturn to her mouth. She was joking with me, teasing me.

I relaxed, smiling at her and asked, "Is my youth a concern for you?"

She waved her hand, dismissive, and settled back in the chair. The sparkle in her eyes was gone. I found myself saddened by its abrupt absence. I hoped I would see it again during our session.

Being respectful of the client's time and the expense of therapy, I like to begin the session as soon as possible. Having completed the customary introductions, I started by confirming our telephone conversation. "When you called, you mentioned your son."

"Thomas," she immediately volunteered.

"Thomas. And that he had recently passed away."

"Tommy didn't 'pass away.' He was killed. In a plane crash."

"That type of sudden death is difficult for the survivor."

"And it was my fault," she continued, not in response to my comment, but completing her own thought as though I had not said anything. "If it hadn't been for me, Tommy would still be alive right now. A mother is supposed to protect her child, not murder him." She paused, her expression haunted, her confession doing nothing to alleviate the weight of the guilt she carried.

She finally looked directly at me, waiting for a response, perhaps a condemnation of her. It took me a moment to digest what she told me. I wasn't entirely certain how to proceed since I was trying to evaluate how she meant that she had killed her son. While I was fairly certain that she had not personally arranged for the plane to crash, it was obvious that she somehow felt responsible. This situation had never previously come up for me in either my study or training. I knew I needed more detailed information from her.

"Did you talk Thomas into flying that day?" I asked, thinking that maternal pressure to get on the plane might also lead to guilt when the plane crashed.

She smiled, animation returning to her features. "No one ever had to convince Tommy to fly. He was like me."

"Do you enjoy flying?"

"Oh, yes," she replied, warming with enthusiasm to her subject. "Nothing could keep me from it. Not my friends; not my parents. Women were just secretaries when I was a girl, but I didn't care. I was determined to fly."

It was only then that I realized Natalie wasn't referring to being a passenger in a plane. She was talking about flying the plane herself, as the pilot.

For the remainder of the session, I followed that topic of discussion. It was only as Natalie was leaving the office and confirming with me our appointment for the next week that I realized how we had talked about her childhood rather than her initial reason for seeing me.

Natalie shook my hand and looking me directly in the eye said "We'll talk about Tommy next time?" Despite her inflection, it was a statement, not a question.

"Of course," I responded automatically.

"Good," she said. "I'll see you next week."

On my way home that evening, I mentally reviewed what my clients had spoken to me about during the day. Thinking about Natalie, I felt guilty that I had spent almost our entire session talking about her youth. I couldn't even honestly use the excuse that I was getting a base from which to evaluate the actions and behavior that prompted her to see me in the first place. I had become so fascinated by her history that as she spoke, I forgot that she was feeling guilty about her son's death. Every indication pointed to the fact that leaving my office, she felt no better than when she had come in. I briefly tried telling myself that a client often did not feel better after the first session. In all honesty, though, I had to admit to myself that in large part it was because I had momentarily lost track of the both conversation and the reason Natalie was there in the first place.

In the back of my mind, I heard the chastisement of my clinical supervisors. During a session, the only thing that should be the focus of the therapist is the concern of the client. I was determined to fulfill that goal during the next session with Natalie the following week.

At the next session, I did much better, but we still spent that main portion of the session discussing her youth.

While I continued to improve each week, I found myself becoming increasingly intrigued with her struggle to do what she loved, pilot airplanes, in spite of animosity from those whom she would otherwise look to for support and encouragement.

As a little girl, Natalie was fascinated by the skies. She watched clouds as they floated overhead, free of any constraint. She was an avid birdwatcher, but she wasn't interested in identifying them as they sat motionless on branches. She wanted to see them in flight, soaring, gliding, riding on an unseen breeze, unfettered by the pull of gravity.

A few months before her tenth birthday, while she was watching a sparrow dart among tree branches, Natalie saw an airplane for the first time. From her point of view, a large, artificial beast moved effortlessly far above the real birds and disappeared into the clouds. Her attention did not waver as she waited for the plane to reappear. Several minutes after the plane was immersed within the cloud, it emerged, oblivious of anything around or below it, continuing on its way until it disappeared in the distance. Natalie watched the sky long after the plane was lost to sight, hoping to see it return.

From that day on, she tried to read everything she could find about airplanes and flight. At the time there was very little in print, and none of it took women into account. She took that as a challenge, not a deterrent.

By the time she was in high school, Natalie's parents were already putting subtle pressure on her to date, specifically with the intention of getting married. She thwarted their efforts, much to their consternation. Many of her friends were either married, or likely to be married, by the time they left high school. On occasion, Natalie did date, but not with the same drive or need as her classmates.

Preparing for graduation, she was uncertain as to the direction she would pursue for her immediate future. Marriage, or the prospect of marriage, would have provided her with that direction, but it was not a factor in her life. The foundations of home and family seen by society of the time as normal for a girl her age were not available to her. Unmarried, and with no foreseeable change in the near future of that culturally unnatural condition to change, she found herself without focus and virtually no support from family and friends.

As graduation neared, she felt increasingly adrift. Only a chance comment from a friend was able to alter her direction. A relatively new branch of the Military, Women Airforce Service Pilots, WASPs, drew her complete attention. Her childhood obsession quickly evolved into the determination of an adult. At the time she first heard of the organization, she wasn't certain if it meant she might be able to learn how to fly, but it was as close as she felt likely to get.

When her classmates left high school for hearth and home, or perhaps a temporary position as a secretary, Natalie, against the wishes and demands of her family, became a WASP.

Becoming a WASP was everything Natalie had hoped it would be, a fulfillment of her dreams. Beyond her hopes and modest expectations, she was taught to fly. Her time in the sky, free from the pull of gravity, made her earth-bound struggles worthwhile to her.

Every moment in the air was a source of joy and peace. Each of those moments became increasingly precious because in addition to flying, Natalie soon learned another lesson, an unfortunate truth of life. Happiness is not merely the achievement of a dream; Happiness is, in large part, the ability to maintain that achievement.

In the years of World War II from 1942–1945, Natalie served as a WASP. She discovered that defending her country did nothing to end discrimination, bias and sexism. She flew cargo to the troops, finding that she had to be better than the men at anything she did in order to be considered to be their equal. Indicative of her personality, she rose to the challenge and not only did she fly missions but achieved a high enough level of expertise that she also trained other women pilots.

It was during this time that she found out first-hand the extent to which animosity can be expressed. She was raped. It was done as a means of proving to her that she was not as accomplished as the men and, more importantly, that she could still be controlled by the men. No one was ever convicted of the crime, nor was anyone even arrested.

Natalie refused to be intimidated, choosing to stay and continue pursuing her love of flight and her joy in passing that knowledge on to others. The only thing that seemed to shadow her enthusiasm was that fact that the sleeves of her clothing wore out and frayed with an irritating consistency. At the time, she didn't realize that she was walking so close to the walls of buildings that she'd brush against them. It was after the rape and she clung to the buildings for the sense of security she derived from them.

At the end of World War II, Natalie remained in Hawai'i, doing what she loved best: Flying. She was able to secure a position as a flight instructor, teaching not only men, but also other women to fly. It was during her time as flight instructor that she finally fulfilled the expectations of her family.

Natalie got married. Not only did she marry, but she also had a child, Thomas, whose death was the impetus for her to seek counseling in the first place. While she adored both her husband and child, she never lost her love of the skies. Her passion for flight infused her son's early development as, even while an infant, he joined his mother in the skies.

Natalie's husband passed away at an early age, leaving her to raise Thomas alone. Once again, she rose to the challenge. She supported herself and Thomas by working in a military museum and, indicative of her affinity for speed, as a racecar driver, building on the mechanical expertise she acquired as a pilot.

When Thomas became an adult, Natalie was immensely proud of his choice of careers. He was making a living as a pilot. As she neared 60 years of age, she was not content to merely sit and watch television. She began a new career as an interior decorator.

Natalie's indomitable spirit brought her success in her new career. Even so, she never lost her love of flight.

When she was close to 80 years old, she was contacted by a young man who was doing research about the WASPs of World War II and wanted to interview her. She was also able to take part in a local air show. She was given the opportunity to fly a vintage airplane of the World War II era, her thrill of again piloting an aircraft a highlight of her recent years.

Natalie and I spoke on a regular basis for several months concerning her guilt over the death of her son. Each time we spoke, I could sense the struggle she was working through, learning to overcome and deal with yet another turn in the fortunes of her life. In assisting her to focus and concentrate on the rewarding aspects of Thomas's life, I found myself, in ways I had not anticipated, learning along with her how to value a life as well as relationships with other human beings.

Gradually, she came to accept that rather than causing his death, she was a major force in the fulfillment and joys of his life. I saw a change in the emphasis of our discussions. When Natalie first came to see me, her focus was on Thomas's death. In time, her reminiscences shifted and she began speaking more and more about his life. She then progressed to talking about their life together. As her memories of life overshadowed her memories of death, her spirits rose accordingly. In following her journey, she taught me valuable lessons that no amount of course work in school instilled in me.

No words can ever fill the void in a parent's soul left by the passing of a child. As I shook Natalie's hand at the end of our last session, I was again impressed by the determination of her spirit to meet her newest challenge. She had stopped trying to find them. She was learning to accept the life he had rather than the life she hoped he would continue to have.

For myself, I felt a newly found confidence in my own ability to celebrate a person's life, and to help others find that same value, not only in their own life, but in the contribution they make to another person's life. I knew I would meet more clients with issues similar to those presented by Natalie, but through her example I felt more capable of meeting that challenge.

Lost & Found

The term 'home visit' is rather a misnomer in that it includes visiting clients in the hospital. Since I had established my practice, I made a point of offering home visits to my clients who were physically unable to come to the office and therefore it was not unusual for me to receive a request to visit a client in the hospital. From the moment I arrived at the room of my client, Chuck, nothing was as I had expected.

I had met with Chuck a few times prior to the call to see him in the hospital. He was quiet, bordering on shy, a tall man with a distinctive, reassuring voice that would be immediately recognizable to anyone who listened to radio news. He loved his job as radio sportscaster, but he loved his wife and family even more. He began seeing me because of a deepening depression that was associated with his learning he had cancer. What initially impressed me about Chuck was that his depression was not tied exclusively to his reactions to having cancer, but also to what he felt was a lack of support from his wife, Silva.

Never having met his wife during our initial sessions, the image I developed was from his descriptions. Knowing his wife and family would be at the hospital, I felt I had an idea what to expect when I arrived. I was very wrong.

Chuck was in a special isolation room. Before I was able to enter, I had to don a sterile gown and move through a vestibule where the air in Chuck's room could move out, but air from outside could not move in. Two of Chuck's five children waited patiently outside the room while Silva sat at his bedside.

When I entered the room, Silva stood, giving me the distinct impression of a sentry preventing unauthorized personnel from gaining access to sensitive security areas. Her unwavering gaze was accusatory, making it known to me that I had no place there. In his oxygen tent, I was unable to tell if Chuck was asleep or merely resting.

"We're tired. You should leave." Silva's statement was emphatic, leaving no room for dispute. "I can't have strangers here now," she added, in case I thought of protesting her edict. Silva, however, was not my client. I felt no particular obligation to her; and therefore her attempt at intimidation did not impress me.

"I'm here at the request of your husband. Let's ask his permission for you to stay in the room, while we talk."

Silva glared at me, and I was certain that she intended to have me physically removed, but we both turned at the sound of Chuck's voice. Even in his debilitated state in the oxygen tent, the resonance of his radio announcer-trained voice demanded our attention. "She can stay."

I sat down to talk with Chuck, but Silva remained standing, her arms crossed over her chest the entire time I was there. At the time, I was basically able to disregard her as I focused on my conversation with Chuck. He smiled as we spoke, seemingly far more relaxed than I imagine I would have been in his situation. I sensed that his ease was a front, a projected image, the same type of acting he had done for years as a sportscaster for even in his weakened state, he gripped the blankets at his sides with an urgency unsupported by his words and voice.

As I stood to leave, I gripped his hand. "We'll talk again soon, Chuck."

"I hope so, Doctor," he replied, for the first time in our conversation his voice lacking conviction.

I nodded politely to Silva as I went to the door. She walked with me for a few steps. "I hope you're happy," she said quietly enough for only me to hear. "It's hard enough for me without other people interfering."

I stopped and smiled at her. "Good luck to you. And thank you for your insight." I left the hospital room, smiling to myself. I had been honest in my departing words to Silva. Without meaning to, she had provided me with valuable insight into Chuck's current emotional state.

Back in my office, I went over the notes I had made while speaking with Chuck, adding further impressions I had gained during our visit. Without realizing I was doing it, I began reading through previous notes of our earlier sessions.

I remembered the first time Chuck came to my office. The moment he introduced himself, I recognized his voice: deep, resonant, reassuring. I'd heard him on the radio for years, keeping me informed about the activities and triumphs of my favorite sports teams. It didn't take long in our session to find out that it was exactly the opportunity to report things in a positive vein, things like wins, records achieved, personal obstacles overcome, that had originally attracted him to sports reporting and currently kept him involved with it.

Within a few sessions, a fuller image of how that interest developed became apparent. Drafted during World War II, He quickly became disillusioned by the destruction and killing he witnessed. As a journalist, his responsibility was to report on the devastation. Naturally quiet and introverted, he emotionally withdrew even further as an automatic defense against having to deal with his feelings.

As soon as World War II was over, he took advantage of the GI Bill and went back to school. There, he found he was able to combine his love of sports and his background in journalism. He became a sports reporter for his school. He expanded his reporting to the college radio station, where his enthusiasm made even a gridiron defeat take on aspects of heroism in doing better than expected, or emphasizing extraordinary plays.

In his senior year, his life changed dramatically. On a blind date, he met Silva, an immigrant from Lebanon. He was immediately and completely infatuated with her. For Chuck, Silva was everything he felt he wasn't. She was outgoing, exotic, emotional, and assertive. For Silva, she was flattered that he was interested in her and she enjoyed being associated Chuck, who had attained the status of a minor celebrity due to his campus radio show. Their marriage soon after Chuck's graduation didn't surprise anyone.

Silva worked hard on improving her English, slightly insecure about her language skills. She admired Chuck for the ease with which he spoke and derived satisfaction from being with him. Five children later, and they still had a relationship that seemed mutually rewarding and beneficial.

Always a heavy smoker, Chuck developed emphysema when he was in his early 60's. This not only did not hurt his career, but it tended to give his voice an added quality of depth and authority, something Chuck consciously cultivated and worked on. Silva saw it differently. She constantly tried to convince him to give up smoking, insisting that the damage to this throat would ultimately harm rather than enhance his career.

At those times, Silva never added the thing that frightened and disturbed her the most. She was Chuck's wife. She derived her sense of identity through his success. If he lost his job, for any reason, it would also destroy the image she had of herself.

Ultimately, Silva was correct about the effects of emphysema on Chuck's voice. Within a couple of years, no amount of effort or skill on Chuck's part was able to compensate for the deterioration of his voice. He turned for support to the one person he felt would always be there for him, but all he received from Silva was a cool distance.

Chuck impressed me on our first meeting with his determination and tenacity. Becoming successful in radio broadcasting and journalism are not easy tasks, but Chuck knew what he wanted to accomplish, what the goals he established required. He set his mind to the tasks involved and successfully accomplished those goals. Silva was with him through it all, receiving recognition and status through Chuck's work and status.

Then, Chuck did the unforgivable. He became ill. He added perceived insult to imagined injury by having to leave his job. When Chuck turned to Silva for comfort and succor, he found a woman who felt slighted and hurt by his apparent abandonment of her, represented by the loss of the security he had provided for her. When that security and the status of his earlier position were no longer there, Silva felt betrayed, that all of the meaning in her life had been taken from her. Naturally, she blamed the one person whom she saw as being responsible for taking away most of what she valued in life, as well as most of the value of her life.

Chuck's children were already adults with lives and families of their own when he became ill. As a group, they did their best to be supportive and helpful to him, and he greatly appreciated their efforts. However, he looked to his wife for warmth and found only cool hostility.

The children tried to understand their mother's feelings, but they found themselves caught in the middle. Rather than appear to take sides or risk the displeasure of either parent, they also withdrew, concentrating on their own lives and families.

Chuck found himself increasingly alone at the very time he needed his wife and family around him. In the hospital, his voice a faint echo of what I was familiar with from his radio newscasts, he had spoken quietly of not being certain anymore what he was fighting for.

Without trying, my memory wandered from Chuck to Silva. As much as I tried to concentrate on my conversation with Chuck and how to approach the issues he was working so hard to deal with, I kept seeing Silva, standing at the far end of the room, arms crossed over her chest, glaring at me. I felt a slight chill at the memory until I realized the problem Chuck was having so much difficulty with really wasn't his. It was Silva's problem.

The realization placed me in a quandary. The main issues facing Chuck were not internal, but external. His main issue was the increasingly cool distance from Silva. Unfortunately, the issues were Silva's, not his, and she was not my client. Resolving Chuck's problems would be much easier once Silva was able to deal with her own problems. Family dynamics could be dealt with, when the entire family came to sessions. Chuck began seeing me as an individual, and given the reception I received from Silva at the hospital, I did not anticipate that changing in the near future. I decided that in order to help Chuck, I would, somehow, have to convince Silva that seeing me would be in her husband's best interests.

Normally, I don't see clients on more than a weekly basis, but I often make exceptions for those in the hospital. Their emotional status is generally far more precarious and they are dealing with very specific, immediate concerns. That was why I was visiting Chuck in the hospital less than a week after my first visit.

He was no longer in the special room with the unique airflow, although he was still in intensive care, being carefully monitored. I noticed immediately that Silva was no where in sight. Although doing better by every outward sign, Chuck seemed more tired than I had ever seen him.

"It looks like you're doing better," I said as I sat in the chair next to his bed. "How do you feel this morning?"

"Better, I guess."

"You don't sound very certain."

"The cancer's not going anywhere." He took a deep breath, staring at the ceiling for a moment before turning back to me. "I thought it would be different, that's all."

"Different how?"

"Just...different."

We continued speaking for the rest of the hour, and everything we discussed reconfirmed for me that the person who really needed to resolve some concerns was Silva. As a got up to leave, Chuck held up his hand for me to shake. Despite his weakness, his grip was firm and sure.

"If you keep improving like this, you'll be able to go back home very soon." I had checked with Chuck's attending physician on my way in and while his prognosis for a full recovery was not good, there was no reason he could not spend his final weeks or months at home if he felt up to it.

"Thanks, Doctor," he said. "I appreciate your help." There was a hollow quality in voice that went beyond his weakened body.

"Chuck," I began, trying to sound as casual as I could. "I'd like to talk to your wife for a few moments. Would that be all right with you?"

"It's fine with me, but if you want to talk to her, you should ask her."

"Thanks. I will."

As I left Chuck's room, I saw Silva walking in the hall. She was cool, evidently choosing not to voice her animosity. I had decided that in order to help my client, I had to reach her. I seemed to have been presented with the perfect opportunity.

"Good afternoon, Mrs. Haynes," I said, forcing her to pause if simply out of automatic civility.

"Hello, Doctor." She offered nothing more and was about to continue on her way. However, I wasn't about to allow her to leave so easily or quickly.

"Mrs. Haynes, I don't usually do this, but I'd like to speak with you about Mr. Haynes." She paused, her impatience palpable. I motioned toward a couple of chairs and we sat down. She was determined not to allow her veneer falter and said nothing, waiting for me to begin.

"Have you spoken to the physician?"

"Yes." While she remained taciturn, her reply was not as sharp or curt as it had been. She also remained seated. Progress in minute stages.

"Do both you and Mr. Haynes understand the prognosis?"

"Yes." She finally looked at me. The expression I saw on her face was so unexpected that it actually startled me. Any trace of anger I might have imagined I would find was absent. She was deeply frightened. "He wants to come home. He doesn't want to die here."

"He'll need help."

"I know."

"Will you need help once he goes home?"

She hesitated, as if she was trying to determine what she was 'supposed' to say. Finally, "I don't know," was her response.

We spoke for a few more minutes. By the time Silva left to join Chuck in his room, I had a good idea how her feelings had progressed. My primary focus and sense of responsibility was for Chuck, since he was my client, but Silva needed to resolve her own issues in order for Chuck to have any hope of resolving his.

Silva was progressing through the stages of accepting death. With his first diagnosis, she began to fear that she would lose him, and along with losing her husband, lose all sense of her own worth, which she always associated with her marriage and partnership with Chuck. Losing him meant she was being abandoned, and she was angry. In her anger she withdrew, unfortunately at the very same time that Chuck needed her with him the most.

Chuck slowly improved to the point where he was able to return home. Everyone knew he was going home to die. No one knew when that would be. I made one home visit to see Chuck after his discharge from the hospital. At first, I didn't recognize the person who opened the door.

Silva was not the same person I had met in the hospital. She took my arm and led me to the couch in the living room where Chuck was resting. She brought a chair next to the couch for me then kissed Chuck lightly on the forehead. "I'll just be in the kitchen if you need me." She disappeared without another word.

Lying on the couch, Chuck was smiling. He cupped his hand over his mouth and whispered "She's listening. If I need *anything*, she'll be here." Despite being physically weaker than I had ever seen him, he was also happier and more content than I had ever seen him.

"How are you? And not just physically."

"To tell you the truth, Doctor, at first I didn't even want to come home. I was afraid that, well, I'd be alone. You know what I mean. And the first few days was exactly what I thought. She tried, but there was something missing."

"What happened after that? What changed?" I glanced toward the kitchen. We could hear Silva humming. She was definitely a different person from the one I had met in Chuck's hospital room.

"I couldn't make it up the stairs. I felt useless and I couldn't even so much as make it up the stairs. We called one of those chairlift places." He pointed to the staircase, and at the bottom was a chairlift. Smiling broadly, he continued. "The worst point in my life turned out to be best. Silva watched those workmen every minute. She made certain everything was perfect, that everything worked exactly as we...as I...needed it. When we tried it for the first time, she walked up with me. I think that was it. We were in it together, for as long as we have together. We talked, I mean <u>really</u> talked, for a couple of hours after that. We talked about our fears. And you know what? We were afraid of the same thing."

"I don't quite understand."

"She felt like I abandoned her, even if it wasn't my fault. And I felt like I was being abandoned. Even if it really wasn't her fault. We figured since we were afraid of the same thing, then we could work together to overcome it."

I couldn't help smiling back at him. "It sounds to me like you're both very wise, and sensitive to each other."

"Yeah, I guess. But isn't that what the best marriages are made of?"

I couldn't have agreed with him more. A few months later, Silva called to tell me that Chuck had passed away in his sleep. She thanked me for my help. I surprised her by thanking her. She and Chuck taught me that love simply isn't enough unless you're willing to communicate with each other and be receptive to each other's needs. Silva and Chuck were two teachers of mine I will never forget.

Façade

80. In our society, someone who has attained this age is, at best, an object of curiosity, rarely seen, but rumored to exist. At worst, this same person is merely considered old, in many cases any individual worth long since exhausted.

80. In my practice, someone who has attained this age is about average, not particularly unusual in any way. A typical client would be referred to me through a senior agency, or perhaps through a hospital, or even perhaps through another client. At age 80, Sofia was not usual.

Sofia was referred to me by the County's Mental Health Services. She had gone to them for assistance, but they deemed her too healthy to access their services. True, they admitted that she was depressed, but her suicide attempt (in 1945) simply did not seem to be something that was of immediate concern. Sofia was indignant by what she perceived to be discriminatory treatment. She believed she was dismissed without assistance due to her advanced education, a degree in physics from the University of France.

Our first meeting was unlike anything I expected. Her attitude was confrontational, yet in an incredibly subdued way. I felt on the defensive, as if she were testing me, daring me to change how she felt. Her attitude was not aggressive or challenging, but seemed instead as though she was very protective of her depression, finding some degree of comfort and solace within it.

Part of my job is to not make any judgment about the issues that clients bring to me. It is my job to listen, to work with the client to come to terms and deal with whatever issue they have. Even still, I found myself wondering how someone could hold on, with such incredible tenacity, to a suicide attempt of a half-century earlier.

It took only a couple of sessions with Sophia for me to appreciate her determination and tenacity as admirable qualities. However, these same qualities were also what were making it difficult for her to reconcile incidents from decades earlier and let them go. She held the losses of her young adulthood closely, with a fierce possessiveness that I found difficult to comprehend. I saw her life and accomplishments as being admirable and noteworthy. She saw the same things as merely marking time, something to do as she waited to die.

Within this context, her suicide attempt at the end of World War II was completely understandable. Sophia was born in Turkey in 1912, the second-to-youngest child and the youngest daughter of ten children. Her parents worked hard to provide for all of the children. In return, the children, particularly Sophia, developed an intensely strong attachment to the family. The family worked together, for each other and with each other, for their mutual support and sustenance.

It was with the support and encouragement of her family that she went to study physics at the University in France. Upon her graduation, her parents felt that her prospects would be far better in France than in Turkey, so she remained in France, although she wanted desperately to return home to be with her family.

Other than her younger brother who emigrated from Turkey to the United States, her entire family remained in Turkey. Living far from the warmth and support of her family, Sophia felt herself to be alone and never quite part of the life around her. She wanted, more than anything, to rejoin her family. Instead, she stayed in France, honoring the wishes of her parents to work for a better life for herself. During the entire time, she felt increasingly isolated, as though her life were on hold.

I couldn't help recognizing that Sophia's feelings during her time in France were amazingly similar to her feelings during her life currently in the United States, namely a lack of substance and a sense of simply waiting. At the onset of World War II, Sophia's waiting took on an urgency that only added to her sense of isolation.

She lost contact with her family as Germany gained control of the French government. Her feelings of isolation intensified into feelings of desperation since she could only imagine the fates of her family. She waited throughout the War, continually attempting to reach her family, continually receiving only silence for her efforts.

At the end of the War, she finally was able to make contact with her brother living in the United States. Through him, she learned that all of the family in Turkey has been killed. Her feelings of isolation turned to deep despair and guilt. She felt that she should have shared the fate of her family, that she should have been there with them for the comfort and support she had grown to rely on throughout her childhood.

Alone in her lab, Sophia took the necessary steps to be with the rest of her family. She found whatever liquids she could, mixed them together and drank the resulting concoction. By chance she was found and taken to the hospital. She then spent several months in a psychiatric hospital where the staff consistently reiterated to her how fortunate she was to be alive, that her life was blessed in that she had not shared the fate of the rest of her family. Rather than lift her spirits, their words did nothing more than reinforce her loneliness and feelings of loss.

Accepting, at least intellectually, that no one waited for her in Turkey, she immigrated to the United States. She worked hard to make a life for herself, but her feelings of isolation never left her. If anything, the feelings deepened, as she found herself in a new country, knowing no one. She felt she never quite fit in, always an observer, never a participant. It was not surprising to discover that she never married, in fact had never even seriously considered the possibility.

She moved from location to location in the United States, first arriving on the East Coast in the late 1940's. She felt out of place and moved to South Carolina, hoping to find some sense of belonging. By the middle of the 1950's, she still felt as though she did not fit in. In an effort to continue her quest for a place to belong, she moved to Los Angeles. The house she purchased never quite became a home.

Her brother, who had moved to the United States when she had moved to France prior to World War II, provided none of the comfort and intimacy of the family structure she yearned for. He had embraced life in the United States and built his own family. He could not comprehend why Sophia would not establish herself in the same kind of life he enjoyed. He could not comprehend why she held to the past instead of accepting the present and planning for the future.

She filled her hours and days with work and research. The same dedication and determination that kept her feeling an emptiness of soul also gave her the tools by which to excel in her work. Sophia would have stood out in any case, being one of the few women in the field of research physics. By devoting herself to her work as a substitute for what she felt was a lack of substance and connection in her private life, she established herself as one of the top researchers in her field.

The impressive accolades she received did not impress her. To her, they did nothing to fill the void she felt while to her colleagues, she appeared to have everything they desired and felt was important.

Unbeknownst to any of her colleagues, she felt exactly as she had immediately after World War II. She would have preferred to have died with her family.

In the early 1980's, Sophia finally accomplished her lifelong desire to return home. She went back to her childhood village in Turkey. She wanted, if possible, to determine first-hand what happened to her family.

She found, not only her childhood village, but contrary to all realistic expectations, her childhood home. She slowly walked past, joyfully awash in memories of warmth and familial love. She saw people living in the house she still thought of as her home and wanted to speak with them, but shied away, afraid that they wouldn't know enough detail to be able to help, perhaps even more afraid that they would know too many details.

Over the course of the next few days, she made a point of walking past the house, gazing at it as she tried to appear on a casual stroll. During one of her strolls, an elderly man approached her.

"Sophia," he began. "I never thought I'd see you again."

She stared at him, shocked and somewhat uncomfortable at being recognized.

"I'm not surprised you don't know me," the man continued. "I barely recognized you, but your eyes. As bright as I remember."

"I'm sorry, Sir…" her voice trailed off. She studied his face, her eyes widening in surprise. "Barmaht? From down the street?"

"Yes. Although it's been years since I lived there. And you, Sophia. What brings you back here after so many years?"

"I had to know—really *know*—what happened to my family."

Barmaht took Sophia's hands in an effort to provide comfort to the young woman he once knew. "Sad, my dear. So sad. All of them killed during the War."

Sophia couldn't help herself. She began crying, her emptiness spilling out in her tears. "I should have been here with them. I wish I had been able to die with them."

Barmaht looked at her askance. "That would have been their life's disappointment."

Sophia looked at him through her tears. "What do you mean?"

"They were so proud of you. They never stopped talking about how well you did in school, how smart you were. They wanted you to stay in France so that you would have a chance for a full and successful life, something you could never have here. The fact that you were alive gave meaning to them. How could you imagine it would please them to take that away?"

For the first time in her life, Sophia began to see herself from the perspective of her parents. It was the first step on a long road for her. She left Turkey to return to the United States only a few days after her encounter with Barmaht.

Upon her return, she tried to reconcile her feelings of isolation with her desire to honor her family's wishes for her life. She found a rather unique method of expressing her needs.

She instituted a trust fund to be used by individuals who lost contact with family members during World War II and were trying to find each other. In her own way, she continued trying to connect with her family by assisting others in connecting with theirs.

She began a minor career change. She started speaking publicly about her survival in France during World War II, and her feelings about her family, who did not survive. Her talks became popular, mostly due to the fact that her story was substantively different from the expected stories from survivors of the War. In a way, her story was something more people could relate to and understand. The horrors of the Holocaust were so extreme, that no one who had not lived through it could relate to what the survivors recounted. Sophia's estrangement from her family was far more accessible to the average listener; they responded by continuing to request her.

It was Sophia's heart attack that began the series of events that led her to me. While recuperating, first in the hospital and alter at home, she had the time to imagine what it might be like to actually die. More to the point, she had the time to reflect on what it might be like to die completely alone.

Her loneliness became more prominent as she came to the realization that she had created her own isolation. In addition to missing her family, she also felt she had betrayed the hopes that her family had for her.

At that point, she contacted the County's Mental Health Services for assistance in dealing with her suicidal feelings. The agency recommended her to me.

To all external appearances, Sophia was an immensely successful woman in a field where women were conspicuously underrepresented. Speaking with her, I came to appreciate how deceiving appearances can be.

Within the course of our conversations, Sophia helped lead me to the first step in her own recovery. We explored how she can make sense of her life, how she could come to terms with her loss.

Sophia, herself, came to see that by living life fully, making positive contributions to society, doing more for others through the auspices of her trust fund, she was keeping alive the spirit her family valued so much. While she had not died with her family, she was able to keep her family alive within herself.

By the time she felt secure enough in her own feelings to discontinue our therapy sessions, she had impressed me with how much a person can change their viewpoint. Moreover, anyone who has not taken the time to get to know them would have no concept or appreciation of the depth of feelings a person has.

Appearances can be deceiving. A very simply truism, but one that my years of academic study never made clear to me as much as did the time I spent with Sophia.

Less is More

It began as a message at my office from the Public Health Nurse. The nurse's description of the 75 year old woman, named Martha, intrigued me immediately. Here was a woman who sounded like a complete contradiction of terms. She was fiercely independent, yet frightened to leave her home. She was fastidious, yet the Public Health Nurse reported her initial involvement was due to Martha's head lice. I was called in because there may have been issues concerning her ability to physically care for herself, as a result of psychological difficulties.

The area she lived in also seemed to be contradictory. She lived in public housing, something I had the unfortunate experience of visiting in other locales during meetings with previous clients. It was always particularly depressing for me to do home visits in these environments. I thought of these elderly clients, seeing and living in these conditions with few outlets to experience the wealth of life beyond the walls of their homes.

This one turned out to be a conglomeration of buildings that appeared to be only minimally in compliance with any known municipal code. Upkeep was nonexistent and graffiti was everywhere with only token attempts made at removal. Old automobiles in various stages of disrepair or decay, exemplified by an old, rusting Cadillac that was probably incapable of movement, clogged the parking lot. It reminded me of pictures I had seen of war zones. Upscale apartments and buildings surrounded the units of Public Housing, creating a small island of poverty in a sea of conspicuous wealth.

I felt immediate sympathy for Martha before meeting her, something I consciously tried to avoid as it meant I was starting with a distinct bias. Whether positive or negative, it never helped the client to make any assumptions prior to meeting. However, as I walked to Martha's apartment, I couldn't help feeling some tinges of anxiety, and, I have to admit, a bit of fear. I could only imagine how she must have felt living in a place I felt some trepidation about merely visiting.

Martha graciously offered me the only good chair in her one-room apartment. She sat facing me in an overstuffed chair that I'm certain Goodwill would have refused. She very matter-of-factly explained to me that people thought that she was crazy, but she was accustomed to it and it didn't bother her. I've heard this kind of denial so often that it normally set up a red flag for me. Martha was different. Her sincerity had a simple honesty to it that was so genuine, I believed her completely. It was a judgment I never regretted.

She spoke of sounds in the night, of voices almost loud enough for her to understand individual words, of doors slamming, and unknown items breaking. I could easily envision all of it, plus some embellishments from my own imagination. She spoke of lying awake in bed, covered by her thin blankets, ready to jump up and run away but too afraid to move.

Her fears were not the product of an overactive imagination, but rooted in violent reality. She had contacted the authorities about her growing fears, but had been ignored. A week after she had tried to get someone to look into her complaint, her neighbor across the hall was murdered. The woman had been hard of hearing and had not known that she was being robbed until the thief killed her as she awakened.

Martha, feeling vindicated, made a point of talking to the reporters who came to cover the crime about how much and how quickly the living conditions of the units were declining. "Would you like to see?" she offered me.

"Of course." I didn't know what she meant, but I was curious. She brought me an old newspaper from the drawer of her end table. She opened it to the page with the story about the murder, and smiled awkwardly as I looked at her picture.

"I wish they hadn't put my picture in the paper, but they did. Nobody said I could have told them not to print it."

"Did it cause you problems?"

"A little bit. But you know, sometimes it's okay if people think you're crazy. They leave you alone."

Driving back to my office after our most recent session, I couldn't help thinking about her last statement. I was embarrassed that it took me so long to make the connection I needed. She had given me the key. For some reason, her experiences revolved around the desire to be alone. I was determined that the next session with her would be productive because now I felt I had an avenue to explore.

At the beginning of our next session, I broached the subject of loneliness and being alone. She looked at me like I was out of touch with reality. "What's wrong with being alone?" she asked me. I admitted that she made a very a very good point. That, however, piqued my interest. What had caused her to <u>want</u> to be alone, when almost everyone else who came to me was because, in one way or another, they did <u>not</u> want to be alone.

Even as she grew up in a small town in Illinois, she felt separate, apart from others, always harboring the innate sense that no one could quite figure her out. As she talked about her parents, it was obvious that, at least from them, no one had made much of an effort. From her description of them, her mother likely suffered from paranoid schizophrenia and her father struggled with alcoholism. The personal struggles of her parents left little time or room for her.

She learned at a very young age that the best person she had to rely on was herself. She tried to do well in school, sensing that it was the best way that she might eventually leave home and find a better life. Unfortunately, she found school to be very challenging. She often had difficulty concentrating in class. With no support or assistance at home, she worked as hard as she could merely so that she would not fall behind. The fact the she was often ill did not help matters. Only later in life did she discover that she actually had Juvenile Onset Diabetes and her persistent childhood ailments were symptoms that went undiagnosed.

Even if her parents had been more attentive and sensitive to her needs, they were too poor to afford the luxury of going to a doctor. They were too poor to even heat their home. They had no hot water. In the winter, icicles formed *inside* their home. Martha grew up feeling that home was a place to escape from, a place to leave as quickly as possible. She simply did not know how to do it.

Her difficulties in school were solved when she was in the third grade although none of her medical or social problems were addressed in the process. In fact, the solution came as the result of additional hardship. She was forced to drop out of school because she was made to take on the responsibility of caring for her three younger siblings by her parents.

Martha may not have had what some refer to as 'book smarts,' but by the age of fifteen, she had found a way to leave home. She got married. A year later she had a baby daughter. She tried very hard to be a good mother, and with her experience in taking care of her siblings, her parenting skills likely surpassed those of her own parents. While her parents had not set the bar particularly high, she was proud of her daughter and her ability to raise the child.

While Martha was able to develop reasonably proficient parenting skills due to necessity, her only view of marriage came from the role models of her parents. She chose her husband for his ability to take her away from her home. She chose a man whose behavior she was familiar with. Her husband was an alcoholic and for several years she made a further choice to stay with him, mostly because she did not want to return home. She also wanted to maintain a semblance of the idealization of what she thought a family should be.

She wasn't even twenty years old when she accepted the fact that the better life she envisioned for herself was not going to be possible within the confines of her marriage. She took her infant daughter and left her husband. She also left behind her fantasy of an emotionally stable family structure.

Martha was determined that she would not return to her family of origin. With little formal education, she found herself with few options. She took odd jobs wherever and whenever she could. Through determination and tenacity, she managed, just barely, to make ends meet.

Miraculously, she also managed to save a little bit of money. Through a government program designed to assist low-income people to become homeowners, she bought a small house. To further live 'the good life,' she purchased a Cadillac. It was an older one, not in prime condition, but to Martha, it exemplified the life she wanted, a better life than what she had left behind. As soon as she told me about purchasing the car, I understood the importance of keeping the dilapidated vehicle I saw at every visit on my way in to see her.

Not only did she have her own home, but she also married again and had a son. She began to harbor the illusion that perhaps, just perhaps, she might have the better life she had always craved.

It has often been cited in mental health journals that schizophrenia tends to run in families. Martha's family validated the journal articles. Her daughter, presumably like her mother, was schizophrenic. Martha had spent the majority of her childhood trying to get away from her mother. Now, as she desperately tried to get close to her daughter, she found her daughter unable to return the feelings. She was not merely isolated from her daughter, she was in physical danger from her child, something she would never have imagined until the day her daughter tried to kill her.

Her husband, someone she had married more to avoid being alone than from any depth of feeling, left her. She resumed her struggle to make ends meet. This time, with two children to care for, she found it was a losing battle. The house she had felt so much pride in being able to obtain went into foreclosure. The only home she could afford was public housing, an alternative to which she certainly did not aspire. Making matters worse, her children blamed her for their declining fortunes.

Martha was not one to sit back and wait for things to happen. She sought solace and found it in faith, practiced at the local church. She became friends with, and shortly thereafter the wife of, the Minister. She and her children moved out of public housing and, for a while, she allowed herself the luxury of imagining she had finally achieved the better life for which she had searched.

Within a year, reality impinged upon her imagined life in a way that shattered her marriage as well as her faith. Her new husband turned out to be verbally as well as physically abusive. Martha maintained a strong enough sense of identity to not allow herself to stay in that kind of relationship. She left her husband, but the experience shook her faith. Like most people, she held the clergy to a higher standard of behavior.

She returned to what had developed into a necessary evil in her life: Public housing. Her concept of a better life still included the idea of being with a partner. She was soon involved with a neighbor, feeding in to her fantasy of what her better life would encompass. She continued with the relationship even after she learned her neighbor was married. He promised he would leave his wife for her, and she chose to believe him. At least she believed him for a short time.

Her neighbor did, in fact, leave. But he left Martha and moved with his wife without telling Martha when or where. Her children, grown into adulthood, had also left, wanting to put as much distance between themselves and their mother who they blamed for their nomadic, chaotic existence.

"Would you like to see them?" Martha asked me, displaying a distinct maternal pride mitigated by a depth of sadness I had not expected.

"Yes, I would."

She brought me a small photo frame holding a picture of two children sitting on the hood of a Cadillac. The children looked healthy, but there was a sadness in their eyes that I saw reflected in Martha's. She smiled as she looked at the photo with me, a photo symbolizing everything that she valued in life.

"When was the last time you saw them?"

"I really don't remember. I guess that means it's been a very long time."

Martha's anxiety at losing her family and her inability to hold on to the 'better life' she spent her life pursuing expressed itself in rather unusual ways. For one, she experienced the sensation of things crawling on her head. When she reported it, and no physical reason could be found, she was easily labeled crazy by those who knew her. Once again, the names did not bother her. She had become accustomed to hearing them so often in her life that at this point in time they no longer carried any negative association for her.

She also became obsessive and compulsive, which were methods of dealing with being alone and the anxiety she was experiencing. She exhibited this behavior by trying to brush the lice out of her at least several dozen times per day, using a very specific routine. More importantly, she no longer trusted people as easily, quickly, or completely. She became angry at what she thought of as the futility of her life. The decay of the Cadillac she had in front of her apartment paralleled the decline in her fortunes.

Most of my clients come to see me because they have developed non-productive coping mechanisms. Martha, on the other hand, developed what I can only admire as a very constructive method of dealing with the myriad issues with which she was faced. She went out of her way to help other people.

She befriended the elderly, hearing-impaired neighbor who lived across the hall from her. She would do small chores, or go shopping with her and help carry groceries. Sometimes, she would make extra food for herself for dinner, specifically to have an excuse to invite the neighbor over for a meal.

During the summer prior to the murder of the hearing-impaired neighbor, five other people were murdered, all in incidents unrelated to each other, within the housing complex. Martha took it upon herself to become an activist for those living in the complex. She called the city, the county, and the department responsible for administration and upkeep of the building. She complained about conditions on behalf of the residents. She pushed for improvements and general maintenance. This was simply another of her apparent contradictions. On the one hand, she was quite comfortable being alone, but took it upon herself to be the spokesperson for the building. I actually found this to be consistent because even while she spoke out, she did it alone.

By the time her neighbor was murdered, she was well known as someone who would not remain quiet. When she spoke to the press during the investigation, it was because she was already the unofficial spokesperson for the building.

Helping others had another benefit for her. She began, slowly, to reestablish a connection to her faith. She started going to church, not on a particularly regular basis, but when she did not attend services, she made a point of nurturing her relationship with God by reading the Bible and, more importantly, helping those around her.

"God helps those who help themselves," she explained to me during one session when I asked her about her gradual return to a sense of faith.

Without realizing it, Martha had touched upon not only a mainstay of faith, but of self-healing of any kind. We continued discussing her feelings about what she was currently doing with her life. During our talk, she told me that she felt her life had been, overall, fairly successful. Looking around her small apartment in the public housing building, thinking of her decaying Cadillac in the parking lot, I asked her to tell me more details about those feelings.

"Because I've had everything I've wanted, at least at one time or another. I've owned a home, had a family, and raised my children as well as I could. I've even owned a Cadillac. I still do. Not many people coming from where I came from can say that. I even help out other people. It may not seem that I have much, but I don't think that you, with all your education, really understand how much I have."

I thought about that last conversation on my way back to my office. I felt she was right. I could listen, I could try to empathize, but really, deeply understand? I wasn't certain anymore. God helps those who help themselves. People have a fundamental hand in their own recovery. Martha understood that on a basic level even more than I did. She understood how much a little could mean.

I hope one day to have the depth and clarity of understanding about what is actually important in life that I saw in Martha.

Action and Reaction

At the bottom of a relatively steep hill, at the end of a cul-de-sac, the upscale condominium complex appeared isolated from the other buildings on the street. I added the sense of separateness to what little I knew of Samuel, "Sammy" as he insisted I call him, the 78-year old man I was scheduled to meet for our first session.

It was Sammy's daughter, Rebecca, who had called me to set up the appointment. She told me she was concerned about her father's behavior, so different from that with which she had grown up. The kind, generous, caring man she grew up to admire was becoming an angry, bitter recluse. As I parked my car and walked to their unit, I reviewed what I knew, a routine I had found worked very well for me in preparing to meet a new client.

I had already counseled enough clients in Samuel's situation that I was confident I had a sense of the dynamics which were about to unfold. According to Rebecca, he was in poor health due do failing kidneys. He had only needed dialysis once a week to treat his condition. The recent death of his wife of almost sixty years, Leah, exacerbated his condition, now requiring dialysis five times a week. He had moved in with his daughter after becoming a widower, mostly at her insistence because she felt he was unable to properly care for himself. Given his medical requirements, she was correct. It was encouraging to see that he had the support of his daughter, whose concern included the fact that Sammy was reluctant, sometimes even refusing, to go for his required dialysis.

It is an unfortunate reality of life that in the vast majority of instances, one partner of a couple is going to pass away before the other. For the survivor, life is forever altered, and more often than not, for the worse. Especially in a case like Sammy's, where the marriage was of such a long duration, and they were deeply attached to each other. His anger, bitterness, and animosity were completely understandable given the circumstances. The fact that it was being directed at his daughter was an unfortunate aspect of the fact that there were few other people with whom he interacted. As Rebecca described it, when he went for dialysis he was so physically debilitated that he was unable to be awful, mean, and nasty to any of the hospital staff. I had to keep in mind the possibility that she might have been envious of the fact that Samuel was nicer to the hospital staff than to her.

Yes, I knew the situation, was familiar with the basic scenario, and was confident that I could guide the sessions in a productive way. I knocked on the door of the unit and was greeted immediately by several moments of incessant yipping from a very little dog with delusions of huge size and ferocity. Rebecca soon opened the door for me. Yippee ran from the room, searching for others to terrorize while Rebecca led me to the den where her father was sitting on the couch, waiting for me.

"Dad, this is Dr. Fuhrmann," Rebecca began the introductions. Sammy struggled to stand, grasping his walker unsteadily.

I held out my hand to him. "Mr…."

"Sammy. Just call me Sammy," he cut me off abruptly. Sammy was slightly less than five feet tall, emaciated, but possessing a remarkably firm handshake. An oxygen tank was next him, the mask within easy reach.

"Is there anything you need, Doctor?" Rebecca asked.

"No, thanks. I'm fine."

"Then I'll leave you two alone." She excused herself, leaving Sammy and I in the room by ourselves.

"May I have a seat?" I asked, indicating the chair near the couch where Sammy had seated himself.

"Whatever you want."

I sat down, smiling with concerned empathy. Sympathy is relatively easy; something you feel for someone else. Empathy is more complex, requiring you to put yourself in the other person's shoes, not an easy task when you have not shared that person's experience. Sammy simply sat and stared at me. The obviously rocky beginning did not disturb me. It was consistent with what I had already expected, including Sammy's recalcitrant attitude. As Sammy stared at me, it became evident to me that this was a man in grief who was reluctant to open up to a stranger. All I had to do was to get Sammy to tell me how he felt about his wife's death.

Sammy continued watching me carefully. I realized that he was studying me. I shifted slightly in my chair, unaccustomed to being the one under scrutiny.

"How tall are you?" he finally asked me.

"About 5-3."

"I figured about that," he said sagely. "A little guy. I don't have to look up at you in order to look you in the eye. That's good."

I had passed some sort of litmus test. For Sammy, we had begun to bond, not from anything I said or did, but simply for being, as Sammy put it, 'a little guy.' He relaxed as he reached for the oxygen mask, put it over his face and took several deep breaths. He put it down and shook his head. "I never thought I'd have to pay to breathe."

"Things change as we get older."

"Sure do. I used to run around, play ball, even beat up guys twice my size. You'd never guess that now."

"Our health isn't the only thing to change."

"You're right about that. I never used to have nightmares, but I do now. Damn near every night. And it's always the same thing."

"Did the nightmares begin about the time your wife passed away?" I was pretty certain where this was going. I only had to guide him.

"Yeah," he agreed, a bit surprised. "How'd you know?"

"What you're experiencing is not uncommon."

He stopped talking, his eyes tearing up. He leaned in close, telling me a secret. From the moment he opened his mouth until our sessions ended, I never again made the mistake of thinking I had any concept of what the session would be about. "I'm a monster," he confessed. "I killed people, even after they were dead. My wife never knew." He paused, his moist gaze never wavering. "Please don't tell my daughter," he begged.

I assured him that anything said between us would never be discussed with his daughter unless I had his written consent to do so. He then began a story that no amount of study, research, or experience would have prepared me for.

As a young man, Sammy felt the same as the majority of the young men around him: He was physically powerful and certain that he would live forever. Given his short stature, he grew up feeling the need to prove him on the streets of Brooklyn, describing himself as a smart aleck who would take on anyone, but having no personal experience of anti-Semitism. Upon hearing vague stories of the treatment of Jews in Europe during the early stages of the World War II, he and some friends joined the Infantry as their way to right those wrongs by helping to defeat the German war machine.

Sammy and his friends, already looking for a fight, were trained to kill in as efficient a manner as possible, using weapons of power and intensity unknown in Brooklyn. Engaging in his first Infantry action on the battlefields of Europe, Sammy learned something he had not expected. Killing someone, even as part of a regimented military campaign, is still killing someone.

Several times during his descriptions, he would pause and ask "When does killing in a war become murder?" I could see the pain in his eyes, and having to tell him that I simply did not have any answers to those kinds of questions, pained me as well.

"You said you killed them even after they were dead. What did you mean by that?"

Rather than respond to my question, he forced himself up and laboriously made his way to an old trunk against the wall being used as a kind of end table. He opened the trunk, refusing any assistance from me. He spent several moments rummaging through the contents, digging deeply into the strata of accumulated memorabilia. He finally found the small tin box he was looking for.

Once again, he refused any help from me as he made his way back to the couch, balancing the box precariously on his walker. He sat and showed me the box's contents: Dozens of photographs and a Medal of Honor.

"Most people would want to display a medal like that," I observed.

Sammy snorted derisively. "Then they'd want to know why I got it and I don't want to talk about it. Can't be proud of getting a medal for murdering people."

"You're telling me."

He leaned in close. "You're the only one I've ever told. Not my daughter, not even my wife. I've never showed anyone these."

One by one he showed me the photographs. Some were blurred, some under or over exposed, most obviously taken in haste with no thought to composition. Sammy explained that the photographer sent the good prints to be used by magazines and newspapers. He had given the ones that did not turn out good enough for publication to those men in the pictures as a souvenir.

One of the pictures, slightly out of focus and very underexposed, showed Sammy and two other men standing in front of a smoldering tank. Sammy stopped, pointing to the tank. "That's what I mean."

I was still uncertain as to what he was referring to, but before I had the chance to ask, he began his explanation. The words poured out of him, bottled up for so long he had long ago forgotten how much there was he needed to tell, and how much he needed to tell it. He continued talking for the remainder of our session.

The two men standing near him in front of the tank were his friends Lenny and Bill. Lenny was a childhood friend from Brooklyn. He met Bill during basic training. The three became inseparable, drawing strength from each other to face sights and experiences that none of them could remotely imagine in the relative safety of life in pre-World War II United States.

The three of them were part of a unit that had overrun the German lines. Several tanks had been immobilized, or destroyed. Sammy and his friends checked the interior of the tanks, making certain that no German soldier survived.

They pulled dead Germans from the bowels of the tanks. They made a pile of the bodies, and set them aflame. They killed the enemy soldiers, even after they were dead. They posed for photographs in front of their bonfires, completely justified in their own form of vengeance. They then joined the rest of their unit for the next battle.

Time after time, they expressed their frustration and rage upon the corpses of fallen German soldiers, those who were incapable of defending themselves. They spent as much time and effort to retrieve the bodies of fallen American soldiers so they could be returned to their families in the United States and given a proper funeral.

At that point in his recollections, Sammy looked directly into my eyes, his own as haunted as when he had began talking. "Why?" he asked me.

"Why what?"

"Those men we killed. They must have had families, too. We made certain they never went home, but we tried so hard to send our men back. It's not right. Not right at all." Sammy paused for a brief moment, then narrowed his eyes, studying me and my possible reactions. "How about you? What would you have done?"

"I don't know. I've never been in a war."

"You must think it was wrong of me. Evil, to keep those boys from being buried proper."

"That's not for me to say."

He sat back, still watching me, waiting for some type of judgment from me. I had been completely honest with him. I had no idea what I would or how I would react in his situation. I had no right to impose any feelings I might think I would have on him and his actions. Initially, he seemed rather disappointed in my lack of response. He sat back, his entire body relaxing, a faint smile on his face, an expression of relief, not happiness. "You won't say anything to my daughter?" he asked me again.

"Only if you tell me in writing I can," I reassured him.

When I arrived for our second session, I no longer made any assumption regarding what we would talk about. Rebecca led me to the den, but Sammy called from the kitchen for me to join him there. He was in the middle of placing a small cup of fresh water into the cage of a small parakeet named, of all things, Lovey. He manifested little of the stiffness or difficulty breathing that he had the session before. After a few moments of cooing to the bird, Sammy turned his attention to me. "Want something to drink?"

"No, thank you. How long have you had the bird?"

"Lovey here belonged to Leah. I've been taking care of her since my wife died." He made a little kissy noise to the bird and led the way back to the den. As I followed him, I tried to reconcile the image of the old man going out of his way to kiss a parakeet to the young man going out of his way to immolate the corpse of an enemy soldier.

He sat in the same spot on the couch, his oxygen tank nearby. This time, though, the oxygen mask was on the side table, close but unused. He wasted no time. No sooner had I sat in the chair opposite him than he leaned in, ready to continue with his story.

After Sammy and his friends set the corpses ablaze, they would return to the still smoldering remains later that day, or the next day if their unit had not moved on. They made certain that nothing was left that might possibly be used to identify the smoking mass as having once been human. Only then were the three young men satisfied. Sammy would sometimes make a point of holding back, one last act he committed that he did not want to share with his friends. He would find some wildflowers nearby and leave them next to what was left of the corpse, the simple act of compassion for a fallen human being feeling like an act of betrayal to his comrades.

It added to his sense of being as inhuman as they tried to make themselves believe the enemy was. He felt that by not acknowledging the dead soldiers as brothers, fathers, sons, and husbands until they could no longer be seen as human, he was no better than a cold-blooded murderer.

He watched men die throughout the war and felt he should have died, too, as retribution for the sins he committed. Near the end of the war, he was in a foxhole with Lenny and Bill. In the middle of a conversation, they fell silent, killed without warning or fanfare. Apparently, they were the victims of shrapnel blasting into the foxhole from a nearby explosion. Within the span of a heartbeat, he went from having two confidants to being alone with the knowledge of his actions. From that moment until he spoke to me, he told no one of what he had done. He had already judged himself, and had no need of a second opinion. After the war, he hid.

He hid by doing everything within his power and ability to be seen as the person Rebecca had described to me in our initial conversation. He presented a consciously manufactured façade to the world. He was kind, generous, supportive, thoughtful, and considerate. He wanted no one he encountered to know that he saw himself as evil incarnate, an inhuman monster with no right to exist among the living.

He donated money and, more importantly time, to a wide variety of veteran's groups and causes. He volunteered at the local VA hospital. He listened sympathetically to physically or emotionally damaged men recuperating in the wards who needed to tell their stories to someone who would not judge them. He never shared his own story in return.

When I arrived for our fourth session, I was surprised to be met at the door by Sammy. He was not using his walker, and he stood straight, leading the way to the den with a slight spring in his step. His walker and his oxygen tank were still in the room, but against the wall, waiting, but not needed. "I almost missed you," he began. "I just got back from my walk."

"Where did you walk?" I asked, a little skeptical. I still had the sense of isolation since the nearest thing to walk *to* was a grocery store, close to a mile away, uphill from Sammy's home.

"To the store." He explained that it took him a while. He would stop and rest if he felt tired. The entire trip took him almost three hours. He seemed a little surprised by his own actions, remembering that only a few weeks earlier he had trouble walking to the kitchen without assistance and ready access to an oxygen tank.

When we sat down to talk, Sammy was still preoccupied with trying to determine for himself when he became a murderer. When did his training, geared to killing people and receiving accolades for it, become murder and being reviled by society for it. His self-image as a murderer was deeply ingrained, honed by decades of internalization.

I was prompted to ask him a question based on how he chose to live since the end of the war. "At what point," I asked him, "is a man seen as being good when he spends his life helping others?"

The question made him pause, seriously considering his response. In all of his years of self-condemnation, he had not bothered to think in those terms. His brow furrowed in concentration, he finally gazed at me, still determined to maintain his pervious opinion. "I don't think that matters."

"What does matter?"

"The kind of person you are. What others see, or think they see, doesn't change that."

During our remaining few sessions, Sammy continued to improve physically to a degree that I would not have believed had I not seen it. As he opened up to me about his experiences and his feelings about them and himself, his nightmares lessened in frequency and intensity. We explored the idea that someone who truly was a monster would never have had nightmares at all, would never have been bothered or concerned about what he had done or what others might have thought. Sammy begrudgingly accepted the concept, but a lifetime of belief is not easy to dispel.

Finally having found someone with whom he could exhume his nightmares, Sammy wanted to continue our sessions beyond the point where I felt he needed any further treatment. The symptoms that his daughter had presented, and I had observed upon our initial meeting, were no longer in evidence. This point in therapy is often one of the most wrenching for me, as I must leave my clients to continue on their own with the tools I have helped them to acquire. Whereas I had initially thought our sessions would be concerned with helping Sammy work through his grief, I found I had apparently helped him cope with his lingering guilt from decades previous.

Rebecca called me a few months after our sessions ended, thanking me on how miraculous his transition was, all due, she was certain, to his interaction with me. I kept my promise to Sammy, never mentioning to her that my only role was to listen to stories he had not given voice to for half a century, stories he had allowed to gnaw at his soul, stories he had chosen to bear in silence, sparing wife, family and friends from an image he despised.

I have often thought about Sammy. Mostly, I learned from our sessions how much I had initially miscalculated by assuming I knew about a client before allowing the client to say anything. To this day, the extent of my hubris upon my first meeting with Sammy embarrasses me. I also think about how he saw himself, how very different that was from how others saw him. I often wonder how others see me, and how that view coincides, or contradicts, how I see myself.

My time with Sammy always reminds me of a quote from the poet Robert Burns: "Oh, that God would give us the very smallest of gifts/To be able to see ourselves as others see us."

Out of Tune

Calm and comfortable. I knew that Alice, the Administrative Director of the Adult Day Care Center tried very hard to convey that sense to people upon entering the small foyer to her office. She felt it was important for both her clients, and the families of her clients to feel secure and safe in the Center. As I waited for her, I felt she had met her goal, a feeling reinforced each time I had come to the Center.

Alice entered the anteroom to her office, accompanied by beautiful strains of classical music being played in the nearby common room.

"When did you hire the pianist?" I asked, impressed by the interpretation of Mozart I heard.

"That's Rhonnie. You've heard her here before. She's the reason I asked you here this time."

That surprised me. I had received calls from Alice in the past to evaluate one or another of the seniors attending the Adult Day Care Center. I couldn't imagine why she would have me speak with someone who would be far more appropriately dealt with by the Human Resources division. I followed her into her office. "We haven't hired her," Alice explained with a statement that was still not an explanation, as far as I was concerned.

"I'm not certain what I can do to help."

Alice closed the door. Normally a very open young woman, I'd never seen her so anxious about privacy. "I'm very concerned about Rhonnie. She's wonderful, volunteers her time to play piano for the seniors here. But…she's starting to forget things. And she's forgetting more things more often."

There are hundreds of reasons why someone might seem to have a faulty memory. Some might be caused by psychological difficulties, some by physical impairments, some the result of medications, some might be simply the result of too much going on in a person's life and the unimportant things fall by the wayside. Based on my evaluation of Rhonnie, Alice would make a decision as to whether or not to hire her as a staff member. For my first meeting with Rhonnie, Alice allowed me to use her office.

A few moments after the music silenced, a soft tapping on the door preceded its opening. Rhonnie came in. I vaguely recognized her from previous my visits to see other clients and she would be playing the piano for the Center's patients. She obviously recognized me as well. She smiled wanly, as she watched me with politely concealed suspicion.

"Hello. I'm Dr. Fuhrmann."

"My name is Rhonda, but I prefer Rhonnie."

"A pleasure to finally meet you, Rhonnie."

"I've seen you here before," she said. "You talk to the old people." She was very polite, but distant, her social graces making up for any discomfiture she might have had.

At about 65 years old, Rhonnie would be one of my younger clients, so her perception of most of the people I dealt with as being 'old' was certainly valid.

"I'd had some clients as young as you," I said, trying to lighten the encounter. I sat down, hoping she would follow suit.

Rhonnie was not impressed by my attempt at humor, but she sat in the chair opposite from me. "I don't know why I need to talk with you at all. I'm not like them in any way."

"Alice asked me to speak with you. Nothing more. She's just a little concerned about you, that's all."

"What is she concerned about? I just come here to play piano for the old people. They enjoy it. And music always makes me feel…well…as though there isn't anything I can't do and nothing I need to worry about."

"Just between you and me, let's think of our talk as nothing more than appeasing Alice."

Rhonnie smiled for the first time. The moment that our talk became something concerning Alice, rather than herself, she was no longer reticent or unwilling to cooperate with me. I was able to assist her in understanding that I wanted to talk with her so not only would Alice be placated, but that it was unfair for anyone to take one person's word in determining what could happen to Rhonnie. She appreciated that, her entire demeanor relaxing as she felt more respected. We spoke for close to an hour, Rhonnie becoming more divulging as she became more comfortable. We agreed to meet again, this time at her home, away from Alice and any influence that might have on either one of us. While I normally do not do a home visit for someone who is capable of coming to my office, I felt that Rhonnie presented extenuating circumstances that made it more feasible for me to go to her home.

For one thing, I have always felt it is far easier to talk to people in environments in which they feel comfortable and familiar. I learn a great deal about someone by their surroundings and the things they place value on by choosing to keep around them. If nothing else, I can use those same objects to begin or lengthen discussions, discovering more about the person. This is especially relevant when dealing with someone like Rhonnie who may be making a concerted effort to put her best foot forward in a public, or private setting. She may be consciously, or even subconsciously, attempting to cover up memory or functioning deficits. I've found that such subtle subterfuges are more difficult for the client to maintain in their home environment where they are comfortable and feel safe.

On my way to Rhonnie's home, I reviewed what I had gleaned from our conversation at the Adult Day Care Center. An only child, she had grown up in a small town that had little access to musical instruments and less opportunity to learn musicianship. The agility of her mind was apparent from an early age. Her supportive mother enthusiastically encouraged any intellectual expression on her part. She absorbed any knowledge she came in contact with, recalling, sorting, and realigning facts to accommodate almost any situation. She took inordinate pride in her intellectual ability, certain it would provide her the means to accomplish anything she imagined.

I smiled in complete understanding as I recalled her description of her feelings as she grew up. I felt very much the same way, imbuing the conceit of my own intellect with the power to overcome obstacles I might encounter.

Up to this point in my practice when I had dealt with clients who were more or less forgetful, it was a state of affairs that I never imagined as pertaining to myself. For the first time, because I identified so closely with how Rhonnie felt, I wondered what it might to be like begin forgetting, and more importantly retain an awareness that you were beginning to forget.

Rhonnie had told me a little about her continued schooling. Unlike most of her friends, she went to college rather than marry soon after leaving high school. She had no specific major or field of study. Instead, she indulged her active mind by taking a wide variety of classes based on nothing more than how interesting they sounded to her.

It was during her second year of college that she fell in love. The first object of her love was music. She began taking piano in her first semester as a freshman, but the love affair blossomed in her second year. She expanded her repertoire to include other instruments, but she continued with, and excelled at, the piano. She was even making a little extra pocket money by tutoring other students, helping them with their piano lessons. Since someone generally will learn more by teaching than simply studying, her own expertise increased at an almost exponential rate. She was soon giving recitals, playing increasingly complex pieces entirely from memory.

The second object of her love was George, an athletic young man a year ahead of her. They married after a brief three-month courtship. By her third year, she was the proud mother of a newborn daughter. Within a year from that, she and George had added a son to their household.

As the World War II raged in Europe some things became more difficult for those at home. Rhonnie gave piano lessons to help make ends meet. She took a great deal of pride in the fact that she was able to help in a meaningful way. She also took pride in other accomplishments of hers; that she continued in school, working toward a credential to teach music, that she could still raise two children, and that she could still give piano lessons. Unfortunately, George did not share her feelings.

Initially attracted by her intelligence and vivacity, he soon appeared to feel it was a threat to whatever image he had of a stable home life. George wanted a housewife. Rhonnie thoroughly enjoyed that aspect of her life, but rebelled at the idea that it would be the definition of her entire life. They began fighting with increasing bitterness.

Like most able-bodied men of his generation, George was drafted. He was not happy about leaving his wife and young children, but the very qualities that were the basis of his disagreements with Rhonnie also helped assuage his fears about their well-being. Unfortunately, his continued insistence that upon his return, Rhonnie would automatically revert to his vision of what a housewife should be ensured that their conflicts persisted.

When his unit left for Europe, Rhonnie was relieved rather than distressed. Their fight continued up to the moment when he hugged her and the children goodbye. Rhonnie was upset enough that she refused to kiss him in farewell and tolerated his embrace in front of the children.

George's letters, borne in the midst of his anxiety, uncertainty, and fear so common in combat situations, stressed his dreams and wishes for a safe, calm, idyllic life with his wife and family when he returned home. Rhonnie's letters in return were cool and increasingly distant as the fantasy he wove he wove for them assumed a specter of reality she did not want to share. Finally, in response to another of his demands for her to quit school upon his return, she coldly, emphatically stated her intention to remain in school as the basis for her career plans to teach music.

She waited for the angry response, preparing her own defense and counterattack. It never arrived. The next letter she received was from the War Department. George had been killed in action.

I completed the mental review of Rhonnie's history as I arrived at Rhonnie's home three days later exactly at the time we had scheduled. I always make an effort to be on time for an appointment. In my time doing home visits I have found that not only do my clients appreciate promptness, to a certain extent they expect it and I lose a great deal of credibility if I'm late.

I was very proud of myself as I knocked on Rhonnie's door. Even given all of my musings and reflections on my way to her home, I still managed to make it on time. I waited, but no one came to the door. I knocked again, waited, and still received no response. Finally, after ringing the bell, Rhonnie opened the door, a polite smile in place for whoever might have summoned her.

"Hello," she greeted me, very polite, but with no indication of any recognition.

"I'm Dr. Fuhrmann," I said, trying not to make it sound like another introduction. The muscles in her face relaxed slightly, evidently seeing something familiar in me.

"Oh, yes. From the Center."

"Yes. That's right. We had a long talk and had agreed to continue it today."

"Of course. Please come in." She held the door open for me, an act of civil grace, nothing more. There was no sense that she recalled our meeting only a few days earlier or our any of our conversation. She led me to the living room, offered me a seat and asked if I wanted anything. The room wasn't very large, but an older, well kept piano dominated one side of the room.

"I'm fine. Thanks."

She sat in the chair opposite from me. As she relaxed, her countenance underwent one of the most amazing transformations I had ever seen. She smiled, this time the expression encompassing her entire face, her eyes lighting up with the recognition they had earlier been lacking. Her voice became softer, warmer. It was a distinct, but subtle change. Had I not been looking, even hoping, for any change, I would have missed it.

"Yes, Doctor. We had a nice talk."

"You were telling me that your husband died in the War."

"He did," she responded coldly. The skin around her mouth tightened, her eyes narrowing in trying to control her anger, a response, no matter how tightly controlled, I had not expected.

"That must have been very difficult, going to school, raising two children alone." I hoped that by helping her think about how she handled herself, she might be able to discuss where her anger was coming from.

"I remember you said that Alice wanted you to talk to me." Her abrupt change of subject took me by surprise, but I decided that the best way I could handle the situation would be to go along with her.

"Yes. She was concerned about you."

"What's your favorite piece of music?" The question, again seeming to change the subject with no preamble, was abrupt, demanding.

"Well…in classical music, I like Mozart."

"*Eine Kleine Nachtmuzik.*"

"Yes. I know that one."

She stood and went to the piano. She sat at the keyboard and looked back at me. "If I can't remember things, I wouldn't be able to do this." She began playing the piece by Mozart. The room filled with the beautifully played, intricate notes.

I didn't have the heart to mention that recalling something from the past was not an accurate measure of present memory loss or dysfunction. For some reason that I'm not certain has ever been adequately explained, people can recall things from their distant past with astounding clarity and accuracy while not being able to remember what they had eaten for breakfast that morning. Ironically, the recall of past events is often more detailed than it would have been right after the event occurred.

The piece ended. Rhonnie turned to me. "You see? Can you do that? You don't understand me and neither did George!"

She ran from the room, crying. She seemed angry, and a little frightened, but I no longer trusted my own reactions or interpretations. I remained sitting, not certain what I should do. I began rethinking what I had done and said, wondering where I might have misjudged her reactions. Therapy is often a matter of timing questions and responses and I definitely felt my timing had been off in this case.

Within a few moments that seemed to me more like hours, Rhonnie returned, gently holding a small ceramic kitten. She was calm, lovingly caressing the ceramic as though it were a living animal. Before I had a chance to stand, she sat on the couch near me.

"That's a beautiful figurine." I was grasping for something to say that I hoped would not further upset her.

"Thank you. George gave it to me before he left."

"That was a long time ago," I said, still hoping I wasn't saying the wrong thing.

"Yes. It was." She remained calm. I felt more relaxed and ventured to continue our conversation. Now, though, I was as interested in her feelings about George as in her feelings about losing her memory.

We spoke calmly for a little while longer and agreed to talk again. I specifically mentioned memory, again appealing to the notion that our talks were merely to placate Alice at the Center. To my surprise, Rhonnie added that she wanted to spend some time talking about George.

On my way home, I reviewed everything that happened. I realized I was disturbed by the entire encounter, and could not quite put my finger on why. I had dealt with clients whose memories had begun to display signs of deterioration to one extent or another. I had dealt with clients who had become angry and had directed that anger toward me. Talking with Rhonnie was somehow different. I puzzled about it until our next session.

I called Rhonnie to confirm our appointment, but she was not at home and I left a message telling her she needed to call me back before I would drive to her home. Less than a half hour later she called back, seeming to remember our appointment. I had the hunch, though, that the message I left triggered her response in calling and she might still not remember we had an appointment, or why. When I arrived at her home, it once again took several attempts for her to come to the door. She answered the door wearing gardening gloves and an apron smudged with garden soil. This time, admittedly to my surprise, she recognized me immediately and recalled our planning to meet. She had simply lost track of time as she was in her back yard doing some gardening. She invited me to come around to her garden and I followed her.

She took great pride in showing me the plants, explaining the kinds of special care each plant needed.

"Next to music, gardening is my love."

"What is it about gardening that you enjoy so much?"

"It's like music."

"I've never heard of gardening described like that."

"I'm surprised. They're the same thing, really. With music, you take nothing and create beautiful sounds for everyone to hear. With a garden, you help beautiful things to grow from nothing for everyone to see."

With a grand, sweeping gesture, she indicated all of the plants in her garden. I couldn't help noticing that even given her care, some of the plants were dying, probably from lack of attention. The dedicated attention she paid to the garden probably only happened now when she remembered, something that seemed to be happening with less and less regularity.

We continued talking as we walked back into the house.

"How did you feel when you received the letter from the War Department about George?"

"I was so angry. At the Army for taking him. At him for dying. I loved George. I didn't love that he tried to make me give up my music, but I still loved him. But when I think about it, I was angriest at me."

"At yourself?"

"He got my last letter."

"You can't be certain of that."

"Yes, I can. If they die before getting your letter, they send you the letter back. I never got it back. And I said terrible, horrible things to him. I even lied to him. I told him I didn't love him anymore. And then he died."

She paused, looking through me rather than at me. "I remember every word of that letter, the way my hand looked as I created each word on the paper. I remember it all so clearly, with so much detail."

This time, she looked at me. "Doctor. Why can't I remember yesterday?"

On my way home after agreeing to meet again the following week, I finally realized why my meeting with Rhonnie disturbed me as much as they did. I identified with her in a way I had not identified with any previous client. For the first time, she had demonstrated a recognition that her mental facilities, her primary definition on herself, were deteriorating and she was unable to halt the inexorable process.

I couldn't help wondering what I might be like at that age, how I would feel to see a part of myself that I valued so highly slipping away, being aware of the diminishment, and being powerless to stop it.

The next week I called to confirm our appointment. Rhonnie was, as usual, politely graceful, but could not recall that we had agreed to meet. Undaunted, I knew Rhonnie was still capable of accomplishing some of what we had excepted to achieve when I first began seeing her. I suggested that we talk about how she felt about her husband.

She was thankful that I would talk to her about something that happened to her so long ago. I had come to the conclusion that we could accomplish little more of value concerning her current memory loss, but we could use the time in which she did remember the past to help her, for the first time since George's death, deal with some of her grief and guilt. Even though she could no longer accurately or predictably access the present, she was still able, and anxious, to come to terms with her past.

We met for another six sessions, during which Rhonnie faced and finally began to overcome the anger she felt toward George, and herself. She agreed with my recommendation for a dementia evaluation by a medical doctor. Unfortunately, the prognosis was that there was nothing reversible in her condition, although with the assistance of certain medications, the progress might be slowed.

With her permission, I gave Alice my opinion of our sessions. Given the ongoing deterioration that Rhonnie was experiencing, Alice agreed to admit Rhonnie to the Center as a client, but allowing her to continue with what she loved: bringing music to others. Alice thoughtfully incorporated the music as a part of Rhonnie's ongoing therapy.

It was several months before the next time I visited the Center. Rhonnie was still playing the piano, but now, as Alice had arranged, she was one of the clients of the Center. Alice said it seemed to help Rhonnie when she played for the others, and even though she sometimes played the same piece two, or even three, times in a row, she played with the same skill and enthusiasm each time. The other clients appreciated the music that Rhonnie brought into their lives. They smiled, their bodies moving to the chords, rhythms, and melodies that Rhonnie seemed to bring effortlessly into their lives.

With Alice's permission, I stopped by the day room to watch Rhonnie as she played. The music was beautiful, and the expression of serenity on Rhonnie's face showed how much she still loved being able to bring music to others.

I can only hope that, if my memory ever fails me, I can still find a way to bring joy into the lives of others. I can only hope that I, too, can find something in life that will continue to give me a sense of contentment and meaning.

Till Death Us Do Part

"It's a suicide pact."

"A what?" I asked automatically, even though I had heard perfectly well what George had said.

"A suicide pact," George repeated patiently, smiling slightly as though allowing me in on a private joke. No matter what the intentions of the client may be, I do not take such pronouncements as a joke. Completely aside from any personal feelings I may have concerning suicide, I am legally and ethically bound to take such things very seriously. I do not take this obligation lightly.

The legal codes of the state where I practice mandate that if I have reasonable suspicion that a client may do harm to him or herself, I am legally obligated to break client confidentiality to contact a crisis intervention team or psychiatric hospital in an attempt to preserve the client's life. The vast majority of clients are unaware of these statutes so I need to inform them of the limits of confidentiality prior to our first session and the possible ramifications of the disclosure of any such information to me.

As I do with any new client, I clearly explained this to George and Helen before sitting down with them and beginning our first session. Furthermore, I have my clients sign a form acknowledging their understanding of these limitations of their privacy. George and Helen had signed these forms not thirty minutes earlier. I had always harbored the thought that at some time this dilemma would present itself to me.

I immediately went into what I can only describe as 'suicide assessment mode.' I had to assess the lethality of the comment. Doing this meant delving into what exactly George meant by the comment, how serious it was, did he have the means to do it, and how likely he was to do it. In short, was there a plan of what to do, how to do it, and did the means exist to carry it out.

"So tell me," I began casually. "Because I'm not entirely clear about what you mean. What, exactly, do you plan to do?"

They looked at each other, obviously taken aback by the thought of having to actually do something about their idea. "I always thought we'd just die together," offered Helen quietly.

"That's it," agreed George. "I just can't imagine life without her."

"Okay. That's a sentiment I can certainly understand and appreciate. But I'm still not entirely certain what you feel that means for you. Can you help me out a little? Just be a little bit more specific."

They looked at each other, then at me. They seemed at a loss as to what to say. George, who had been the more outgoing by far, was thoughtfully quiet.

"Well," George finally began, speaking more slowly than he had since I met him. "I really hadn't considered anything that far ahead."

"It's not a set plan," Helen added. "Just a way we thought neither of us would have to be alone. I can't imagine what that'd be like. I don't want to try."

"Okay," I said, relaxing. "That's something we may want to touch on at some other time." I was reasonably certain that the lethality of George's original comment was minimal. For them, it seemed to be a romantic, *Romeo & Juliet* ideal of doing everything together, even dying.

I was able to concentrate on the remainder of the session, confident that their pact was more fantasy than reality. It was an idealistic dream, not a set plan of action. As I drove back to my office from George and Helen's home, I reviewed the session in my mind, filling in several temporary blanks with some of the background I had gotten from Helen when she had originally called to set up the appointment.

Almost three weeks earlier, a Home Health Care nurse had referred Helen to me to talk about her depression. Helen took the referral, called about a week later, but was insistent that it was her husband, George, who needed to talk with someone. Despite her own ailments, diabetes and recent surgery to remove a small, benign tumor from the underside of her jaw, she dismissed her own feelings in deference to her husband. Even during our short conversation when she called it was clear that she was quite depressed, a fact she readily admitted. Her reason, though, was concern for her husband, not because of any of her own difficulties.

On very rare occasions, I had seen clients similar to Helen and George. They had been childhood sweethearts, married each other in their early 20's, and now, in their late 70's and married for over 50 years, they had never really been apart.

Once the last of their three children had grown, married, and moved from their home, they had only each other to interact with on a daily basis. For the majority of people, this 'empty-nest' syndrome, new-found proximity, and enforced intimacy places an enormous burden and strain on a relationship. The tenuous bonds that once united a couple begin to fray, often unraveling beyond repair. For a rare few, the bonds deepen and strengthen, creating an interconnectedness of intimacy and mutual empathy. The two psyches intermingle to the point where a third is created, greater than the sum of the individual parts. They genuinely feel each other's sorrow, pain, elation, and content. Interviewing one is much like interviewing the other. So it was with George and Helen.

Helen had called hoping that I might be able to help George with his depression. His well being was her focus, her primary concern. Her own feelings were minimized, mentioned only in passing, and then only because she had an innate sense that his depression was somehow connected with her own recent physical ailments. Their thoughts and feelings were so intimately, deeply interwoven and dependent upon each other, I found my greatest challenge initially was to determine for myself who the client actually was.

Driving home from our first session, I still was not entirely certain if George or Helen was my client. The difficulty each was experiencing was empathy for the pain of the other. Since I had originally spoken with Helen, I was seeing George only because she wanted me to talk with him. Certain he would not agree to see me on his own, it was her idea that I should come and see her, inviting George to join us to help provide background and the perspective of someone close to her.

She warned me that he would not appear to be depressed, but she knew that he was, and would be reticent to speak about it. When George came into the living room to join us with their Border Collie, Lad, padding loyally in his wake, he was laughing and made a point of telling me some jokes he had been working on. The outgoing man who shook my hand had little resemblance to the depressed individual I thought I would be seeing. Helen had told me that he was a sometime comedian, wrote his own material, and occasionally had the opportunity to perform some stand-up. When she spoke of him, it was with pride in his accomplishments. There was no hint of disappointment in the fact that he held only odd jobs, his career being mainly to try to bring enjoyment to the lives of others. The simple joy she felt in being near him was evident in every move, gesture, and expression.

As the session had progressed, (and after the suicide pact announcement), George's levity diminished slightly. He began to show some of the signs of the depression that Helen knew was there and had brought me in to try to assist with. He gently held her hand, really just having his hand in contact with hers, as though not being in contact with her was not only beyond his comprehension, but physically impossible for him.

George made it very clear that he was there only because he thought he might be able to help Helen through the depression she was experiencing due to her recent illnesses. He seemed to have no idea that Helen had brought me in with the understanding that he was the client and it was his depression, not hers, that I there to assist with.

The day before our second session, I reviewed my notes about the first session with George and Helen. I sincerely hoped that my wife and I would some day have the same level of interconnectedness shared by George and Helen. I have to call it "interconnectedness," for it was something far deeper and more profound that mere emotional intimacy. For a brief moment I understood with frightening clarity the sentiment behind George's off-hand declaration that they planned to die together.

Just as it seemed physically impossible for George not to be in contact with Helen, it was mentally and emotionally impossible for him to exist in a world where she could not share in that existence. She had been ill, but it was George who experienced the depression of dealing with ill health, more profoundly because it meant he was seeing Helen suffer.

Helen was the same in reference to George. From everything that I could see, she was not particularly distressed over her illnesses. She was rather pragmatic and viewed it as merely part of growing older. What was debilitating to her was seeing George suffer.

If one were to die, a significant portion of the remaining partner would also die. The only way to circumvent this predicament would be for both of them to pass away at the same time. The only way to ensure that would happen would be a suicide pact. I put the thought from my mind a moment after it formed.

During their second session, I began to further understand that their feelings went beyond their obvious connection. There was a distinct sense of pride in the fact that they were independent, able to do things on their own. Neither wanted to have that independence taken from them. Neither wanted to become a burden on their children. This seemed to lead me right back to the concept of their suicide pact.

They had their fates wrapped up in a neat little package. They understood the potential problems and had devised an efficient solution. As much as I think I understood their perspective, all of my professional training, not to mention my personal belief system, railed against their conclusions.

As I reviewed my notes from our second session, one thing began to stand out for me. Their unmistakable devotion to each other was a part of, and major contributor to, a deep fear of being alone. The depression each one exhibited in his or her own way was in part a reaction to an unspoken fear that, if one should die, the resulting loneliness would be unendurable. That fear, real and tangible for each of them, was perhaps something that I could help them work through.

A few days before our third session, I received a call from Linda. It took a moment for me to make the connection of who the caller was. Linda was the youngest daughter of George and Helen. She was informing me that George had passed away and that she hoped I would keep my appointment to talk to Helen, who needed the therapy more now than before.

At first, I didn't quite follow, and asked how George was taking it. In my mind, he was the healthier of the two and my immediate impulse was to think that Helen, still recuperating from recent surgery and in generally weaker physical condition, had passed away. Linda politely corrected me. "I'm sorry," I said, trying not to stammer an apology in my embarrassment, silently vowing to myself to pause for a moment before responding.

Linda was unsurprised. "Don't worry. Everyone's been saying that," she told me. She gave only scant details about George's death, continually falling back to: "I'll let Mom tell you about it."

I arrived at Helen's for our scheduled appointment. The woman that answered the door was barely recognizable as the woman I had met and spoken with on two previous occasions. She was utterly calm and composed, observing all the required civilities, but any hint of joy was absent from her demeanor. Their dog, Lad, shadowed her every move, keeping just out of her way, its tail never rising.

She spoke of the funeral arrangements, admitting that she felt she was going to need a great deal of help. She said that she was glad her children were around. They were helping her not only with the funeral, but also with a myriad of small things around the house. Basic, life-maintenance things like laundry, shopping, and cooking. She deeply appreciated their assistance.

At one point, about half way into the session, she paused, looking at me, though I had the distinct, rather eerie impression that she was not seeing me. When she finally spoke, that impression was reinforced by the fact that it seemed as though she was speaking to herself rather than to me. "It's a little surprising how calm I feel."

"You haven't mentioned yet how he passed away."

"They were going for a walk." She placed a hand on Lad's head. He leaned against her. She stroked his head absently a couple of times, then folded her hands back in her lap. Lad put his muzzle up, gently nudging her arm, but when she didn't make any further move toward him, he stretched out on the floor by her feet. "He took Lad for a walk every day. Sometimes twice a day because he said that Lad needed the exercise." Lad looked up at her at the mention of his name, but didn't rise.

"Then what?"

"He never came back. The paramedic said he had a heart attack. Lad stayed by him, crying until someone came."

"The paramedic told you?"

"Yes." For the first time in a while, she looked directly at me, and this time I know she was seeing me. "He said 'goodbye' when they left, just like he always did. But that's not the same as having the chance to say 'goodbye.'"

At the end of our session, her demeanor changed from the numb, methodical recitation of facts and agendas to something I found myself uncertain how to negotiate. She reached out to me and took my hand. "Doctor," she said quietly, her eyes never leaving mine. "I don't know what I should do now."

As the professional, the one that was being paid, if not to provide the answers, at least to be able to guide a path toward the answers, I had no idea how to tell her that I didn't know what she should do, either. Not during graduate school, nor even during my clinical internship, did I ever feel so utterly unprepared to deal with a client. I finally relied on the one thing that cannot be taught, or trained for. I relied on my intuition. First of all, I felt compelled to spend more time before I felt comfortable leaving her.

During our first session, I had taken George's almost casual remark about their suicide pact very seriously. Before I left, I needed to know what Helen thought of it now that the subject was a reality. She had a choice to make. She could live that idealized fantasy, or somehow learn to negotiate a new reality.

"To be honest, I don't know what you should do right now. I do know what you and George discussed, though."

She let go of my hand and sat back on the couch, once again folding her hands in her lap, deep in thought as she considered the question. I was relieved that she did not have an automatic response for me.

She took a deep breath, sighing heavily before replying. "It seemed to make such sense at the time. It was just words, then. I didn't think how it would actually have to be done."

I felt myself beginning to relax. Actually formulating and then carrying out a plan to kill yourself is quite different from just saying you'll do it in theory.

She took another deep breath. Once again I had the impression that she was addressing herself rather than me. "I only hope that I have the courage for it," she said as she finished her thought.

That wasn't the conclusion I wanted to hear from her.

"Helen," I began. "Do you remember what I explained to you and George before our first session?" She lifted her shoulders slightly, which I took to mean that she didn't remember. "This would be one of the few times when I am required to break confidentiality," I continued.

Her expression did not change in any way. This did not appear to be a good sign. "If necessary, we can have you checked into a hospital. It would only be for a few of days, of course. For a little observation," I concluded.

"I'm not going to do anything," she reassured me. "It's one thing to talk about it, but I don't know how I could possibly do it."

For some reason, that no matter how often I've thought about it and tried to pinpoint the specific thing that triggered my reaction, I have been unable to identify whatever it was that made me feel that she was not being truthful with me. It was my intuition again, and I felt it profoundly, deeply, with every fiber of my being.

This presented me with another dilemma. In order to ultimately serve the best interests of my client, I had to question and challenge her credibility. I found this to be extremely difficult. I had always had a deep respect for my elders, which was one reason I found myself working so well with my chosen clientele. Furthermore, in the present circumstances, she could easily withdraw more, feeling a betrayal of the trust and the comfort we had worked to establish. Repeating some of the same tactics I used in our first session to determine the degree to which she might actually commit suicide, I began to have a very different feeling than I had gotten that first day. Yet, there seemed to be enough of an ambivalence of suicidality that I felt I could play that up and capitalize on it.

I carefully choose every word I said in an effort to convince her that the best thing we could do for her would be to check her into a hospital. We both knew she was lying when she continually assured me she would do nothing toward fulfilling the pact she and George had made. Neither of us said anything about the pact or even referred to it. Very slowly, in emotional increments that would have been impossible to pinpoint with any certainty, she eventually agreed to my suggestion to allow herself to be hospitalized.

With her permission, we called each of her three children, all of whom agreed without hesitation, to come to the house and accompany her to the mental health hospital. She stayed there, under observation, for the next several days, attending grief support groups and continuing with individual psychotherapy sessions with me.

She was allowed to leave for the funeral services the next week in the care of her three children. She stayed at the hospital for another week, at which time the general consensus amongst the professional staff was that she had progressed enough to be allowed to go home. Following her discharge from the hospital, I continued to see her on a weekly basis. Her mood gradually improved as she worked through her grief. In response to this improvement, we reduced the frequency of her sessions to every other week, then further reduced them to only once a month. Eventually, we agreed that she had reached the point where she no longer needed continuing treatment. She promised to call me if she ever felt the need in the future. By this time, I trusted she would follow through, but I did not hear from her again.

While I felt that I had certainly taken the correct course of action on her behalf, there was still a small, quiet voice that wondered if I had done it for Helen's best interest, or my own. I wondered, in my own life, how I would react if my wife passed away unexpectedly. I like to think how I would react, but I had to admit that I really didn't know. I didn't know if I could, or would even want to, live with that depth of loss because in a very real sense, I simply could not imagine the reality of that kind of loss.

I knew it had been essential to confront her when she was being less than honest with me about her desire to end her life, but that did not assuage the ambivalence I felt about doing it. Thinking about it merely brought me back to the same question of whom I had done it for, Helen or myself. I was legally obligated to do anything and everything possible to preserve her life. For me, this was as much an ethical consideration as a legal requirement. Was following the letter of the law and my own conscience a service to her, or a disservice? Truthfully, I wasn't certain.

A few months later, I received a call from Linda. This time, I immediately recognized the voice and connected her to Helen. She told me that since Helen had been home from the hospital she was a little quieter than she had been before, but that she was not only taking care of herself, she was helping to take care of the grandchildren. In fact, she would often ask to take care of them rather than merely agreeing to a request made by one of her children. She was walking, sometimes twice a day, with Lad because he needed the exercise.

Linda seemed happy, and relieved, as she told me how Helen made certain to tell the grandchildren stories about George, allowing them to get to know their grandfather, even when he could not be there. She was happiest when she was telling the grandchildren about George, a way she found of keeping him alive for herself by keeping him alive for others. She told them his jokes, which everyone seemed to enjoy. Helen had recently told her that: "George is still doing what he loved to do. He's entertaining other people. He can still make them laugh."

She even told Linda that she was glad she was still alive, because if she weren't, the grandchildren would never have gotten to know George. As difficult as it sometimes was for her to continue on her own, she found a purpose by sharing her image and memories of George with the next generation. One of her greatest joys came when she heard one of her grandsons playing and telling a friend of his, "My Grandpa has this joke." In fact, she had told it to her grandson a few weeks earlier, emphasizing that it was George's joke. The children's laughter was the best therapeutic treatment she could possibly have received.

Without meaning to, Helen taught me to trust my own instincts and intuition when faced with a difficult situation. During my sessions with Helen, I was forced to admit to my own feelings (psychotherapists may refer to them as countertransference) that occurred any time that I began to think of what I would feel or planning to do in her situation rather than what she was feeling or intending to do.

Working with this client also gave me the opportunity to explore my feelings about confronting an elderly woman in despair. Ironically, I believed that my role was to be protective of her perceived fragility at her time of greatest loss. Like many 'younger' people, I neglected to appreciate the resilience of the human spirit when it inhabits an elderly body.

Change of Pace

"Adapt or die."

These three words are the essence of evolution, whether physical, emotional, or biological. Darwin started a revolution in every science by his theory that adaptation leads to survival. This concept has been applied to everything from microbes to species to social policies to economics. In psychology, there is even an adaptation of this concept. It deals with the coping skills acquired during the normal process of aging.

Simply put, as one matures and takes on the greater responsibilities and roles of adulthood, one adapts to the circumstances in order to survive, and ultimately prosper. There is also an addendum that has become a truism in aging studies: As people get older, they become more like themselves.

It works this way: As a person ages, there is gradually less reliance on the veneer of coping skills that have been acquired during his or her life. Perhaps a mild-mannered individual, who had to exhibit a hard edge to survive in business, once retired, no longer needs to maintain that façade and therefore appears to have changed, when in reality he has simply become "more like himself."

This apparent conflict between the need to adapt and the tendency to remain intrinsically who you are wound up being the fundamental reason why Douglas came to see me, although neither of us recognized that at the time. He was 85 years old, married only three years earlier to Teresa, a younger woman of only 65. He was depressed, not for himself, he assured me, but because Teresa was depressed, recently seeing a therapist on her own. She was becoming more vocal regarding what she considered to be difficulties in the marriage. "I'm here," Douglas began, "because my wife thinks I've got a problem. She's even talking about divorcing me."

I couldn't help but agree that there definitely seemed to be a problem, especially if Teresa was serious, rather than merely lashing out and saying whatever she felt would elicit a response. I watched Douglas closely, his tightly clasped hands folded on his lap the only indication of his tension.

He stood out among my clients for several reasons. He was older than my average client by almost 20 years, yet appeared to be in his late 60's. He was tall, lean, very fit, and extremely alert and intellectually challenging. Upon meeting me for the first time, he questioned me in detail regarding my approach to therapy as though conducting a job interview, or a cross-examination. I would soon find out that he was highly skilled in both areas. My initial reaction was of a man who was, perhaps, overconfident, and in control of every aspect of his life.

He had been a businessman for his entire adult life until the age of sixty. He found he was having difficulty dealing with his business associates, so he quit. At a time of life when most people are planning their retirement, he went back to school to become an attorney. The law school initially balked at admitting him. He believed that they felt that a man of his age would not benefit from the rigors of law school, let alone live long enough to seriously enter into the practice of law if he should manage to graduate and pass the bar examination.

He fought for the right to attend, citing age discrimination. He not only did well in his classes, but he passed the bar exam on his first attempt. He joined a law firm, only to find that he had difficulty getting along with the other lawyers at the firm. Rather than quit, he simply opened up his own law firm.

So far, he fit very nicely into my own preconceptions of an older individual who "becomes more like himself." As he aged, he was less and less constrained by the social conventions requiring conciliation. He naturally found himself having an increasingly difficult time getting along with fellow workers. He solved his dilemma by isolating himself even more from the very people he was unable to interact with on a meaningful basis.

This inability to meaningfully interact with other people not only applied to his business life, but perfectly described his home life as well. He had grown up in New York of Eastern European heritage, marrying at a very young age to Christine, a woman picked out by his mother. He and Christine never connected, on any level, but to please both his mother and his wife, he remained married for close to fifty years.

He and his wife had two children, with whom he had a close, emotional attachment, but his relationship with his wife was a disaster from the beginning. Their children never had any idea that there was anything amiss. Douglas and Christine never fought in front of their children. In fact, they never fought at all. They simply did not care enough about each other to engage in any interchange.

Throughout their fifty years of marriage, Douglas had numerous affairs, always with younger women whom he felt would not actually want him, never having any trouble with dissolving the relationship when it might possibly progress into something that carried even the slightest emotional weight. For fifty years, it seemed Douglas never developed the interpersonal skills necessary to maintain a meaningful relationship. It was always easier for him to quit and begin something new than to work at developing any depth. It was clear to observe how he repeated the pattern in business that he learned in his interactions at home.

He always harbored an underlying guilt concerning his affairs, but pressure from both Christine and his mother compelled him to remain married. Christine tolerated the affairs because she derived material satisfaction from his success in business. His mother simply would not hear of a divorce in the family.

He stayed married until his mother died.

After having lived to please others for his entire life, he divorced Christine, left the law firm he had recently joined, opened his own firm, and earnestly began an effort to break down the compartmentalization of his life. His children, well into their own adulthoods, blamed him for breaking up what they envisioned as a solid marriage. He began losing the only personal connection he had.

There was one additional component that tipped the scale for him. He told me about it during one of the early sessions. He sat quietly at first, his fingers lightly grasping the arms of the chair. His eyes were cloudy, but he made no move to wipe the excess water from them.

"It was my granddaughter Jenny," he finally said, then paused again.

"Your son's daughter?" I prompted.

"No. My daughter's daughter. She would have been 23 on her birthday the next month." He paused again, but I had a sense of where he was going. By this time, I was certain that he was unable to see, yet he still refrained from drying his eyes.

"Would have been?" I prompted again after waiting a few moments for him to continue.

He nodded before speaking. "It was a stupid accident. A drunk driver ran a red light. She was a passenger in the car that the guy hit. I guess they never saw him run the light. She was killed instantly."

"I imagine that's one of the worst things to happen, to lose a child…or a grandchild." I hoped to draw him out, to have him share more of his thoughts and feelings. His feelings, though, led him in a slightly different direction from the experience of grief that I expected.

"Instantly," he repeated. "Life can change, or end, in a moment. And you never know when or why." He took a deep breath, but I could see that his eyes were now clear, with only the remnants of moisture. "I was already old when she died. I could go at any time."

At that point in his life, he seemed to have made a conscious choice to change how he dealt with the circumstances and events of his life. A few years after his divorce, he met Teresa, a woman close to 20 years his junior and as dissimilar to Christine as two women could be. Teresa had been born in Santa Fe, New Mexico, a full-blooded Navajo. She was warm, caring, opinionated, emotionally and physically demonstrative, and not a bit afraid of standing up for herself and what she wanted from him and from their relationship.

The insistence on Teresa's part to work on the relationship was the very thing that led to greater difficulties, as Douglas had never had to learn or develop those fundamental skills. He was accustomed to a wife that said little and expected nothing from him. He had never had occasion to experience himself as being lovable, and was not quite certain, in fact was almost suspicious, as to why Teresa would love him.

After the first few sessions, it was very apparent to me that the man who sat in my office describing a life of uncompromising rigidity, who dealt with people and life events within an extremely limited frame of reference, was no longer that same person. Douglas had transformed himself into a man willing to accept the fluidity of situations as they presented themselves to him.

It's one thing to accept a situation in life. It's quite another to deal with it in a productive, meaningful manner. Douglas lacked the necessary skill set to interact outside of his strict parameters. He was willing to try, but had no idea how to proceed. Thus began a series of events whose outcome I would never have foreseen.

Douglas had decided to accept the fact that Teresa loved him. He made the conscious choice not to try to understand why, or to attach some mysterious ulterior motive to it. The only way he was able to conceive of a way to express the love he had for her was to give her something of himself, something he had never cared enough, or bothered to give to Christine. He gave his time, his companionship, and his attention.

Unfortunately, he had no frame of reference to guide him concerning the limits and boundaries that couples subtly negotiate with each other. He had no idea that this particular form of intimacy is something that is negotiated and worked out at all. He fully expected that she would reciprocate completely, measure for measure. Without realizing it, he was becoming greedy, demanding more and more of her time and emotional availability.

Teresa, though, was close to her family and felt that Douglas was forcing her to make a decision between him and her own children and grandchildren. She was not pleased, and let him know about it in no uncertain terms.

During our sessions in which he described the confrontation, he struggled to maintain a modicum of control. His anger seethed beneath this thin veneer, a primal, passionate, powerful emotion he had never felt toward any woman before. He was scared, and yet there was a sense of exhilaration that he felt anything so deeply. "It doesn't make any sense," he said. "I love her, and yet sometimes, I feel so frustrated that I don't know what to do."

"It doesn't have to make sense. It simply is."

He shook his head, not understanding. After half a century of feeling nothing for his first wife, he had considered that lack of emotion to be normal and was therefore surprised that he was capable of feeling so much for his new wife. He also failed to realize that feelings, especially deeply passionate feelings, could have both positive, and negative, ramifications.

At any moment, I expected him to retreat to a position that was familiar to him, something that had worked for him on every occasion in his life. I expected him to quit and simply start again at something else. This time, it was me who was surprised. He said he wanted to, and would, do anything necessary to save his marriage. Normally, at this point, I usually have the partner come in for a joint session, so that I can gain a fuller insight into the interplay and dynamics of the two people involved. I explained to Douglas that in this case, since Teresa was seeing her own therapist on an individual basis, I did not feel that would be appropriate. However, if she and her therapist would agree, then a joint session with him, Teresa, her therapist, as well as myself might work. That way, neither client would be in a position of feeling that their issues were being marginalized because each client would have their own therapist there, serving as their client's advocate.

Douglas agreed wholeheartedly. The next step was to finalize the logistics with Teresa and her therapist. Willing to do anything to make this work, Douglas agreed to meet at the office of Teresa's therapist, Joan. I had worked with Joan on other previous cases. After obtaining permission from both clients, Joan and I spoke beforehand to familiarize ourselves with what we planned to do in the joint session.

The session began well enough, as both Teresa and Douglas stated their own issues. Generally, at this point, even though the clients are verbalizing their feelings, things are still on a more or less superficial level. They progressed rather more rapidly than I had anticipated, probably because each felt comfortable with the arrangement.

The depth of feeling each had for the other was manifesting itself in negative, blaming accusations of uncaring or thoughtless demands. It was apparent to me that no one who cared as little as was being stated would bother so much, and so loudly, to be a part of someone's life.

Finally, Teresa, unable to verbalize her frustration, said the one thing guaranteed to undermine Douglas's stand. "I can't take this anymore," Teresa said. "I want a divorce."

Rather than argue, or fight, or return with an attack of his own, he began to cry. The thought of losing her was more than he was able to process in any verbal way. Once again, Douglas behaved in a manner contrary to my expectations, even though by this time I felt I knew him. I was learning how little I did know him.

Teresa's response was also surprising. From Joan's reaction, it appeared that she was also taken slightly off guard. Rather than reacting with the expected maternal instinct to attempt to 'make it better,' Teresa backed away. She wanted a strong partner and his crying she felt was an indication of weakness. Douglas's reaction scared her.

"It's the fighting," Douglas offered after a brief, uncomfortable silence. "I don't want to fight."

"Neither do I," agreed Teresa.

"But," Douglas lamented, "it's how we always end up."

The comments from both of them gave Joan and me something to work with. Whatever conflicts they had were exacerbated when each one became entrenched in their own positions. From the perceived righteous safety of their own biases, they could launch attacks at each other, fully secure in the knowledge that their own position was correct.

We gave them some homework to do in preparation for our next joint session. We assigned them the task of compromise. If a conflict came up between them before the next joint session, no matter what the subject matter, each one was asked to give up a part of their position, to compromise in some way.

Douglas and Teresa left, both agreeing, albeit somewhat grudgingly, to carry out their assignment. Joan was confident that Teresa would make the necessary effort. I was less hopeful concerning Douglas. I was familiar with his history of leaving a situation that was not progressing in the manner he felt it should. I could easily envision him reacting in a way that was true to his innate nature and personality.

There was one individual session with Douglas before the next scheduled joint session with Teresa and her therapist. I was not surprised when Douglas began talking about the fight they had. Teresa was planning to visit her children and grandchildren. Douglas had some time off and wanted, in fact expected, that she would spend it with him. This was not a new fight, but merely a continuation of their most emotionally loaded, ongoing conflict.

"You and Teresa made an agreement to compromise," I reminded him.

"I know," he admitted. "We did."

I was honestly taken by surprise by his almost casual remark. "What kind of compromise did you reach?"

"I went with her to visit her family."

"Was this her idea?"

"No," he answered calmly, discussing something as though it had no more explosive potential than a decision to take his coffee black or with milk. "It was my idea."

"It sounds like an excellent idea. What made you think of it?"

Finally, Douglas spoke like the man I had come to know. He was pragmatic, logical, to the point. "I wanted to spend time with her. This way, I got to do that on the drive over and back. She got to spend time with her family like she wanted. And it gave me the chance to get to know her family a little better." He paused, considering the results of his proposal. "Her kids are fine people, but the grandkids are real young. I guess I'm getting a little too old to keep up with kids that young. It wore me out."

"So it worked out well."

"Overall, I guess it did. I mean…we didn't fight."

The next joint session was a revelation to me. Never, in my years of training or counseling, have I had a client who was so willing to work on issues and improvement. Douglas did everything that was asked of him, coming up with his own improvements whenever he could, working diligently on every assignment given to him.

It wasn't perfect. There was a lot of backsliding and false steps, but he never lost his focus or direction. If something didn't work, or didn't work the way he had thought or hoped, he tried something else.

His enthusiasm and dedication to solving his own issues and working on building a better relationship with Teresa were inspiring. Teresa demonstrated her love for him by working every bit as hard as he was in creating a nurturing relationship that they could both benefit from.

Adapt or Die.

Through Douglas I learned to confront my own biases and subconscious prejudices. Of all people, given my training and vocation, I felt I would be the last one to harbor preconception of what an elderly client would do and how he would behave. I was firmly convinced that Douglas would simply become more like himself, yet here was a man committed to changing himself for the better.

By adapting himself to his new situation, he was able to flourish in ways no one would have thought possible. He inspired not only Teresa, but without realizing it, he inspired me as well. When I am confronted with a situation in life, I now consciously think about what I will do. Will I react by becoming more like myself, or will I adapt, change, and grow?

More often than not, I find myself choosing adaptation. This book is a direct result of that. Only a few years ago, I would never have attempted anything of this magnitude, in an area so foreign to my own frame of reference. Inspired by Douglas's example, I decided to adapt to new circumstances in my life and try something that would, no matter what the outcome, be a source of growth for me.

In a society that marginalizes its older populace, I can only hope that others will find inspiration from my elderly clients. I know I certainly have and my life would be far less rewarding without them.

978-0-595-40597-8
0-595-40597-5